Spiritual DNA

Spiritual DNA

A Method for Spiritual Enlightenment

By

Abraham Aizenman

Translated to English by

Taylor Ffitch

"Everything that happens has an explanation
and is for the good"

Abraham Aizenman

Letter of Recommendation

ד"ר רפאל גרנות Ph. D N.D ברפואה טבעית

יועץ מוסמך לעניני בריאות בכל ענפי הרפואה הטבעית

בדיקת שיער לאבחון מחלות הגוף

כל אדם הוא עולם שלם

✔ בדיקת שיער מדוייקת.

✔ התאמה אישית של מזון ותרופות.

✔ מאמן: שמירת בריאות, ריפוי מחלות, ספורט וזוגיות.

www.drgranot.co.il | 050-4182887 :נייד | 03-5796717 :טל | בני ברק :משרד

ב"ה

אל כ' אייר 2018

אשר תשפ"ט

הסכמה וברכה!

הסופר הנגרם שליט"א נין ל' ה"ן גאון עולם כתב:
ר.ג.ה רוחי והד"א אולי להבב. הישואני וללמוד שיוו,
התחולמ/ לוגדל בלבב בורה ולנדא אלא גהאמאו!
הוקין יארות ואצבודה ש כל חבא הוישמר א הקבלה ולאחל הסלו ולגדהם ני
א הים המקום יהודה ל"ב ואשר בהקל- לפ הסולם, הקוין והקולא
'נ לנאוד וגם לקטתקון לקיבל א אצא נב' האו חבאה פויקק.
ולגדהם לנד תוה הישרל וד מאני וני' וני' אא בכך.

מבקר ולל שיקן לגדל בסוה ודחואד הקבל.

הרב נתן ברבן שליט"א
נ"י ברק
0525-919743

(Translation of the letter of recommendation for this book)

Dr. Raphael Granot N.D PhD in Natural Medicine

August 2018 – Elul 5778   B"H

<u>Consent and Blessing!</u>

The writer Abraham Aizenman allowed me to review the book he wrote: *Spiritual DNA* and published. I was very much impressed by the content, written in a clear and orderly manner filled with wisdom! The reader can understand the idea and the elevated thought raised in its content.

The author, Abraham [May his light shine] awakes, expand and elevates all the hidden wisdom of Kabbalah and particularly from the explanations of Rabbi Yehuda Leib Ashlag zk"ll - Baal HaSulam. The reader may learn and may as well experience curiosity to take upon himself to learn this ancient wisdom.

Abraham learned hidden Torah from me, and I am proud of it. I bless him and wish him to continue expanding in Torah and in the wisdom of Kabbalah.

Rabbi Raphael Granot shlit"a

Bnei Brak

0525-919743

www.drgranot.co.il | 050-4182887 | 03-5796717

Table of Contents

Spiritual DNA

Prologue

I would like to thank the almighty Creator, may He be blessed, for giving me the strength and support to complete this book.

As a child, I was always a skeptic who paid little attention to religious or spiritual topics. I was diligent, and had more interest and ability in math and abstract thinking, the sciences, social sciences, and art.

I was born and raised in Bogota, Colombia, by Jewish parents. In search of a better life, my father left Poland when he was twelve years old, just as Hitler came to power. My mother, daughter of Romanian immigrants, was born in the mountainous Andes region, center of the Colombian coffee plantations. She and her sisters were educated by strict teachers in a catholic school run by Swiss Franciscan nuns. Influenced by her strict education, which emphasized and affected her spiritual life, my mother developed a healthy habit of daily prayer. I don't remember a single day when I didn't see her pray.

I attended primary and secondary school in the Colegio Colombo Hebreo (CCH, the Hebrew school). After two years studying basic engineering at Los Andes University, I moved to the Israel Institute of Technology—Technion— to continue my studies in systems and computer science. I have wonderful memories of my years as a university student. There was little spirituality, much Bohemian life, music, rumba, and more.

We were a Colombian Jewish family, although not very religious. For many years, until I was 15, I was part of a liberal scouts group. On our camping trips we would sit around a campfire to sing, talk about life and transcendental topics like the purpose of life, the desire to reach some kind of spiritual understanding, to understand the meaning of life, what made us happy, the socio-economic system we lived in, politics, the Middle East, art, and so on.

From a young age, I began to question the reason for my existence and the meaning and purpose of life and of death, with an intense spiritual desire.

At 22 I had an experience that permanently awakened my interest in spirituality. One night, as I was sleeping, I had a strange and intense sensation of the presence of my Aunt Olga—my grandmother's sister—who lived to help others. At this time, she lived hundreds of kilometers away from us in a different city, but that night she appeared clearly in my consciousness. I couldn't see her with my eyes, but my body physically felt her pull me towards her by the arm, as if she was asking me to go with her. I woke startled, scared, but with a feeling of having experienced something real. It took me some time to go back to sleep. In the morning, my parents told me that my beloved Aunt Olga had died that night, "coincidentally" at the same time that I had experienced my contact with her.

I then began to ask myself if there was something that, without having physical or magnetic mass, communicates between or unites people. Some kind of network which, though imperceptible to our five senses, exists and joins us to everyone, no matter how physically distanced we are from another person, unlimited by time or space. I asked myself if it was possible to outline something that would function like a spiritual system.

Spirituality became an important topic for me, and began to draw my attention so particularly that I began to study everything related to it, trying to be realistic and immune to fantasy, without believing in ghost stories and other non-scientific inclinations.

I studied, and continue to study today, with the support of different teachers who opened doors for me in many areas related to the spiritual word: Jewish law, Kabbalah, mysticism, astronomy, and gematria.

Now, forty years after that experience, I can understand and value the importance of the spiritual system, the parts that make it up, and how to make daily life filled with peace, tranquility, and happiness. I began to understand that everything that happens to us is for the good, and for a positive reason, and that it comes from the spiritual system that controls our lives and that is composed of and includes everything relating to the world around us: family, friends, colleagues, and so on, as well as public or private entities that influence our lives both directly and indirectly.

What problem does society face?

In many parts of the world, today's problems are starting to perpetuate the fear and desperation that are, unfortunately, undermining our existence. This leads to changes in our lives.

Civilization is sinking beneath worldwide economic, environmental, and social crises. The capitalist system doesn't provide solutions, but rather contributes by increasing our anxiety, weakening us and making us lose sight of the horizon.

Is there something we can do as people and in our relation to others to achieve the best possible life under the conditions of this agitated 21st century?

This book proposes a method to attain and transform our lives into something of value, with hope, passion, integrity, optimism, charity, love, gratitude, justice, liberty, and order.

This doesn't mean a life without problems, because, as my good friend André Assin (RIP) said, the only person who has no problems is already dead.

While we live, we need to correct ourselves. Things can be changed for the better, improving the present.

Spirituality in My Life

As part of my family's customs, we were taught to perform acts of charity, to give money to the poor, give away clothes we weren't using, give food to the needy, and so on. I remember that, when I was 11 years old, a boy about my age came to beg. It was cold out, and my mother told him to wait a moment. After a few minutes, she gave him a sweater that I really liked and that I was still using, despite it being old. The sweater was already a little tight on me. Without much thought, my mother gave the sweater to the boy. I immediately asked her to give him something else, not this sweater that I felt so attached to. Then my mother told me, "You should never get attached to anything material, all material will pass away one day, including our bodies." This phrase pierced me on the spot.

At the age of 25, divorced after a year and a half married in an awful relationship with my ex-wife, and with a daughter as a product of that relationship, I began one of the most difficult times of my life, in which I suffered a depression that lasted 5 years. It caused me to get sick and absorbed all my energy, making my life miserable. My mind clung to a pattern of complaints; I blamed myself and my ex-wife; self-pity and resentment were part of my life in those days.

I saw counselors and psychologists, but they didn't help much. I finally realized that if I didn't forgive myself or my ex-wife I would not have a happy life. This conclusion made me understand that the future was not something I could control, so I should act in the here and now. Forgiveness came slowly.

I learned that anger served no purpose, but rather the opposite: it strengthened my false ego.

Today I recognize that egoism never comes without shocks and discord, and I understand that my mind cannot forgive, but only my soul, my interior, my being. I delayed several years in approaching my internal peace, which helped me to better understand the spiritual system and which, with time, brought me total immunity from depression, which I have never felt again, ever!

When I was 33 years old I immigrated to Canada in search of a better future. At that time, for the first time, I started to study topics related to the Jewish tradition, including the *Talmud* and the Kabbalah.

I began to plot the first points in the map of the spiritual system and to gather relevant facts.

Five years later, I took a vacation to Bogota, to visit my family and friends. I met with my good and dear friend Pepe Rodero, a Spaniard living in Colombia. After not seeing one another for a long time, Pepe's eye was caught by a splendid, expensive shirt I was wearing and that I had bought a week before the trip. On a whim, showing little shyness and a lot of *chutzpa* (boldness, impertinence), Pepe asked me to give it to him; he argued that he loved it and that I should give it to him. His request took me by surprise because it was the first time I had worn the shirt. It fitted me very well, but I thought, "How many times has Pepe asked me for something? To make a long story short, I gave him my new shirt. He was grateful and put it on immediately. I stayed in my undershirt without much discomfort, as the weather was nice. To this day I can see Pepe's enchanted smile and joyful face. It was gratifying to me and I felt happy to see my dear friend happy. It was the last time I saw Pepe. I returned to Canada, and three months later I learned that he had died of a heart attack at 40 years old. I often ask myself, how would I feel if I had denied him the shirt? For me it was an opportunity to live my present correctly, giving love. His smile and his happiness are recorded in me forever.

It was the beginning of an appropriate, more structured education in my search for a clear, basic path that would outline any given human being's spiritual system. I learned to observe and analyze from a spiritual perspective. I searched for the spiritual identity that could offer us a key to a better existence. I became a quiet spiritual pioneer, a spiritual investigator.

In my free time, I studied cinema as a hobby. As a student I wrote, directed, and produced a few short films, one of which was about spirituality. On a very tight budget I filmed a 15 minute-long movie about spirituality called *Beshert* (Twin Souls). The film appeared in several international film festivals, and was awarded a prize at one. *Beshert* is a love story based on the Kabbalah, and it says that "40 days before a child forms in a woman's womb, the person who will be their *Beshert* is already chosen." The movie tells the story of a young man's search for his twin soul. (It can be found on YouTube or rented from the Canadian Filmmakers Distribution Centre in Toronto, Canada).

Next, I spent five years living in the United States, until the end of 2000, when I decided to finally move to Israel. The years I spent in the U.S. and Canada provided me with various spiritual revelations.

Although it is not very spread out, Israel possesses the energy and the eternal blessings for all its inhabitants to be happy and feel satisfied. As is written in the sacred scriptures, the land of Israel was given the divine capacity to make all who live here happy. This fact is undoubtedly true.

I believe Jerusalem is the place with the most powerful spiritual energy in the world, where a person's soul vibrates with the most clarity and quality. I was lucky to be able to visit many places around the world that are recognized as vortexes of positive spiritual energy. They say that in these places a person's soul vibrates on a higher level. A few I can mention, among others, are Sedona (Arizona), Banff National Park (Canada), Machu Picchu... a positive spiritual energy emanates from these places that connects people's souls. But there's nowhere like Jerusalem. If you have never visited, you should go. It will make you feel something "special".

My Pain is Your Pain

On many different occasions in life we have felt pain, malaise, anguish, worry, disruption, fear, offenses, sorrows, and disappointments.

I have experienced these feelings innumerable times. They are terrible situations. They are part of life, yes, but if we want to keep living we must never accept defeat, never!

The question is: how to be happy? Or at a minimum, how can we feel neutral, with neither pain nor glory? Feeling good helps us to correctly evaluate our situation, and accordingly be able to make decisions calmly and using emotional intelligence. Occasionally, pain comes from seeing the pain of someone close to us whom we love. In that case, their suffering can cause us pain even stronger than theirs, leaving us not knowing what to do.

After many years of trying and testing practical "solutions," such as going to doctors, taking medication, psychological treatment, alternative therapy, rabbis, spiritual counselors... I reached the conclusion that the answer to the majority of the questions was in the management of our spiritual system, the spiritual entity that governs the individual and the social environment. I call it a spiritual "system" because it functions like one, and in this book the workings of a model of the spiritual system will be explained in detail.

The Message of this Book

The purpose of this book is to establish a method for understanding and achieving spiritual force for the individual and their interactions with others.

Additionally, here we want to lay out a way of thinking, of analysis, and behavior that allows daily life to be enjoyable. Once a person begins the road to spiritual illumination, they can join with other people with the same goals and together spread benefits to society in general. The daily spiritual work will contribute to an evolution toward a better, "illuminated" world, in harmony with nature, for us, our children, and future generations.

This book is the result of my studies, searching, and observations. I hope and desire that its content reaches many people who are starting their path to recognize their spiritual system and put its teachings into practice at the individual and group level within our families, friendships, and the society we live in.

It is my desire that the path toward spirituality and progress in comprehending the spiritual system described here will stimulate readers to be conscious both of our spiritual life and material life. The adoption and practice of some of the basic concepts mentioned here will very probably also bring good health, wealth, true love, and time to enjoy a beautiful life. I have confidence that this book will help us to approach a state of enduring knowledge for true comprehension of our spiritual environment.

Foundations of the Proposed Method

This book is based on notes written in my Kabbalah classes. The Kabbalah is based on the study of the book the Zohar (splendor), written in Aramaic by Rabbi Shimón Bar Yohai ("Rashbi") in the 2nd century CE. For thousands of years, up until the last century, only a limited, select group of people came to understand and spread the Kabbalah, given its esoteric content and its complex, abstract text.

It was just in the 20th century that Rabbi Yehuda Ashlag (1885-1954) known as "Baal Hasulam" (In English, the owner of the stairway, wrote his master work: *Commentary on the Zohar*, which took him ten years to finish, between 1943 and 1953, and includes a translation of the *Zohar* from Aramaic to Hebrew, as well as extensive interpretation.

This interpretation is written in such a way that it finally opened the doors of the *Zohar* to all of humanity. Thanks to his commentaries and to others of his books, Rabbi Yehuda Ashlag helped us to understand the *Zohar*, through a tiered approach which allows us to gradually assimilate details until we finally understand it.

His commentary on the Zohar provides us a "staircase" by which we ascend and access the secrets of the Bible. This is how he earned the name "Baal Hasulam."

In this book terms and ideas are cited that are already known and established in the works cited in the bibliography. I use them in order to introduce the topic of spirituality in general and the Kabbalah in particular. My contribution consists of proposing a spiritual model or method for success on the path to spirituality. The book also contains original explanations according to my understanding, interpretation, and experience of the spiritual system, all in a common language for easy understanding of the topic.

Many books have been written about spirituality, but how is this book different?

First: because it is the product of my search, my point of view and experience. I want to share with the general public the way to be "happy and satisfied with what I have in the moment." This doesn't mean that I don't want more, exactly the opposite: yes I want more, but I live happy with what I have.

Second: The method I present offers a structured, tiered process for the management and recognition of the spiritual system, which, when we practice the model, will channel us and help us to achieve success in any objective we set ourselves.

Third: it will outline a clear synthesis of the path to follow in any spiritual project or work. The majority of books on the topic aren't clear, and sometimes are very far from precise.

Fourth: this book shows that the result of spiritual work can be measured and quantified. The influence that an individual or group has on others can be calculated and measured clearly. The proposed spiritual method works and can be implemented at any time, as long as certain necessary conditions are fulfilled. The spiritual system described in the *Zohar* is an exact science.

An important point that this book presents is a clear push to reach the spiritual goal along with a team of people and society in general because, as we can see, it is the only way to improve humanity's existence.

Scope and Focus

The solution laid out here will impact those who are ready to start or who have already started on the path to spirituality. The proposed model is a system for spiritual growth and achievement in us, a spiritual model that defines its parts and activities. We explain what the spiritual system runs on, what its internal and external processes are, what results it will bring, and its modus operandi.

This book is directed at people who look for answers and feel a desire for spirituality (which is usually called "the point in the heart," a term coined by Dr. Michael Laitman in his books). This book will help innovative people who are capable of achieving interior transformation and of being open to incorporating and adopting new types of thought, analysis, and operation in the spiritual field.

We have applied a scientific and mathematic lens that allows certain relationships to be defined among the different components of the spiritual system. The underlying focus of the book is to present the spiritual system. Although it is a science—that's why we use some technical terms—we endeavor to make it easy to read and understand, and that the model developed here leads us to understand our spiritual system. There will perhaps be readers who may feel intimidated by some mathematical terms or terms from computational systems. I recommend that those readers let themselves flow with the text and concentrate on the content of the spiritual model.

Most likely this book will help those who are curious and beginning to perceive spirituality to understand how the system functions.

Additionally, it will give them a tool to understand where and how to nourish the soul, the spiritual part of an individual. The concept of soul is defined and explained in detail later on. Sometimes reading a book about spirituality, even without internalizing its ideas, is enough for the reader's soul to assimilate them intuitively.

You will find this book to be friendly. In some parts, it is written in the form of coaching, like teaching; in others it is more informal. We should try to read it for personal meaning, because each individual has their own spiritual aspect that controls, recognizes, and is aware of them. There are some paragraphs we recommend taking breaks while reading, so as to internalize them better. Others will explain common concepts in the Kabbalah in simple words for easy understanding.

Spirituality is the reason for and the nucleus of every religion, but this book isn't about any religion or tradition in particular.

From time to time we will cite fragments of the Bible and other Jewish sacred books, but only in order to deepen, widen, and strengthen the meaning of the spiritual model in question. In the book some specific practices will also be discussed, such as prayer.

Because it draws from the *Zohar*, this book is supported by Judaism. What this book aims to do is explain the spiritual system that is common to all people who, though they don't profess the Jewish faith, can feel attracted and inspired to adopt the method described here and apply it to their lives, adapting it to their own beliefs. Furthermore, I propose a structured method—independent of any religion—for the management and recognition of the spiritual system in ourselves, open to all interested people.

I trust that it can be useful in some way for those who search for answers related to their lives, their interpersonal relationships, love, mental health, or other aspects. People with positive natures will find its content valuable for reflection, even if they aren't inclined to apply the rules and suggestions proposed here. If a single reader finds an explanation or small part that illuminates something or solves one of their problems, it will have been worth the effort to write this book.

Some questions, uncertainties and objections will doubtless occur to the reader. I hope that they will be answered by simply continuing to read, and they will dissipate and become irrelevant as some of the concepts are internalized. We want to add that the words and phrases used to express a concept, idea, or notion, have the purpose of advancing debate on the topic.

Chapter 1. Spirituality

Spirituality is a commonly used word these days; I found many options when I searched for a definition. In general, religions have considered spirituality to be a fundamental part of their practices and mystical experiences. Spirituality is the essence of all religions, but it exists independent of them and beyond worship and traditions.

The term "spirituality" comes up whenever we ask ourselves, where did the universe come from? What is the meaning of life? Why are we here? What happens when we die? Why do disasters happen? What is the evil eye? Is there order in the chaos? Why did I have a car accident? What does what I've been shown or what happened to me mean? Why does this person have a disability? And so on.

We define spirituality as the expression of the "divine" part of ourselves that can influence another person or people in reciprocal conditions of mutual self-determination.

When we say "divine," this doesn't necessarily mean anything mystical or religious. When we say "divine" we mean that the person shines with positive energy, feels satisfied and good, creates trust and has a positive influence on those around them through their actions or attitudes.

The practice of religion can help a person to develop and advance their spirituality, but spirituality, or more precisely a person's spiritual system, exists within them even if they have no connection to religion whatsoever.

Spiritual Challenges

The world's development is the result of the expansion of the human ego. By nature, every individual has an ego, which attempts to control and limit the person's behavior. Because of this development, our society has achieved scientific and technical advances that bring answers and services like never before. We live in a completely interconnected world, where information flows ceaselessly 24 hours a day, seven days a week, all over the world.

We have gained many luxuries and advantages from this development, but we also suffer untenable disadvantages which afflict us every day with less space and less privacy. In this network of interconnected networks, the flow of data feeds us all on the same diet of opinions, understandings, and biases. This daily intercommunication causes diversity to contract. Slowly but surely, we are all being trimmed by the same scissors.

In order to enjoy our life's journey, to live optimistically, to be happy with the daily hustle and bustle, and to achieve satisfaction with what we have in the present, we must understand the spiritual system that we control and carry within ourselves.

Ego

The ego is the desire to feel pleasure or satisfaction connected to a sense of personal identity. Sometimes, to the extent that it gives us self-esteem and self-confidence, a certain amount of ego is positive.

Being self-satisfied or self-fulfilled is called egoism. Doing something so someone else gets direct satisfaction is known as altruism.

In spite of thousands of years of ego development and growth in both people and society in general, all of western civilization has yielded disastrous results: environmental contamination, climate change, destruction and abuse of natural resources, crop speculation, growing anxiety, incessant searching for "something," fundamentalist wars, totalitarian governments, theocracies, multinational cartels that control the majority of basic resources, manipulation of the truth in the media for ratings... and other natural and social disasters.

The world is dominated by fear and subjugated by negativity which is a consequence of our egoistic mentality. There are symptoms of collective dysfunction: civilization is heading toward self-destruction, and a dangerous sense of alienation is easily spreading to many people around the world. The sensation of having our privacy invaded is painful. We feel robbed, violated, and powerless. Independence and free thought get rarer every day. We are condemned to be part of this collective insanity as long as we continue to allow ourselves to be dominated by our egoistic mentality.

Egoism is an innate part of humanity. We are flesh and blood, and therefore we instinctively want to get life's necessities. Since our creation, due to our nature, human beings have dedicated ourselves to obtaining and consuming both necessary and unnecessary goods.

Few essentials are necessary for material life: shelter, food, security, sex, and health. Our goal should be to provide this everywhere in the world. But the reality is different. Now, at the beginning of the 21st century and under the political and socioeconomic system in which we live, people strive to gain money, power, and honors, to win titles and achieve knowledge.

We will always want to receive; there is no way to avoid it or to remove this drive, it is innate. The ego will always exist and we will never be able to separate ourselves from it, so we should learn to manage our egos and make them receptive to growth and to developing the Creator's essence within us, thereby making ourselves into people with influence, despite our consumerist natures. We dedicate the entirety of the next chapter to this topic and the concept of the Creator.

We should learn to use the power and weight of our egos themselves to transform them and channel them into helping us to become influential and even altruistic.

In the Bible it is written that man was created in the image of the Creator. In the Jewish tradition, and following their calendar, 5,777 years ago (2,017 years, according to the Gregorian calendar), Homo sapiens recognized their divine soul. Since the creation of the divinely-conscious world, 5,777 years ago, humanity has been constantly moved away from its spiritual realm, alienated from our divine part, generating a spiritual breach between humanity and the essence of the Creator. Meanwhile, we begin to understand the great spiritual loss or harm that we are currently suffering as humans.

During the indiscriminate growth of ego over thousands of years, the world has accumulated goods and riches. But King Solomon's words about life's earthly goods, "Vanity of vanities! All is vanity. What advantage does man have from all things under the sun?" lead us to conclude that the only thing above the sun is spirituality.

Thousands of years ago the world finished its spiritual evolution at the inanimate, vegetable, and animal levels. In the past 5,777 years, we have been developing the human level of spirituality, beginning with Adam, the first man with consciousness of the divine, and passing through different stages up to the current spiritual state.

According to the book of the *Zohar*, of which the Kabbalah is a product, it will take humanity approximately 6,000 years to achieve the state of perpetual spiritual energy revealed in us. This is the time required to correct humanity. In other words, within a maximum of 223 years (before 2240 on the Gregorian calendar) we will reach our goal and perfect our spiritual identity. I say maximum because is not dependent on chronological time—it could be today, with the help of the Creator—but rather on humanity's spiritual activity. When we reach 6,000 years the entire world will experience a state of higher consciousness. This does not mean that it will be the end of the world. The world will still exist, don't worry.

There are two possible paths to bring the entire world to a state of higher consciousness:

1) Normal spiritual evolution, which currently puts us on pace to reach the goal in 6,000 years. In other words, continuing step by step, at our own pace, without any acceleration.

2) Choose the path of the Light, the spiritual path, through the study of the Kabbalistic method, which teaches us how to accelerate the process in order to achieve our goal sooner than 6,000 years.

In the first case, we are simply surviving reactively and adapting ourselves to the natural development of things. In this normal, "slow" way, we will experience suffering, plagues, and setbacks... these scourges balance us and correct us "naturally."

In a civilization driven by the natural egotistical mentality, there is a gap, or difference, between the position our spiritual aspect requires and our actual, current position. This gap includes the accumulated attitudes and behaviors practiced over the centuries that humanity has overlooked, ignored, or failed to correct in our souls. This book refers to this difference between the current position of our souls and the place where we should be (the Creator) as a "spiritual lag." This topic will be covered more fully in the next chapter.

Our minds, in the 21st Century, reflect an accumulation of psychological negativity and a spiritual lag of thousands of years. Humanity's shared ego is known as the "integrated ego," which encapsulated us all and which, at the same time, separates us from one another. When the integrated ego grows in an unbalanced way the Law of Equilibrium (which will be further explained later) is activated, leading to all kinds of disasters.

The wisdom of Plato and Aristotle was for the benefit of their own egos, so that everyone would know how wise they were and how much they knew. Today, something similar occurs, but with money instead of wisdom. For example, despite the vast number of medicines that the pharmaceutical industry puts on the market, the majority are ineffective or do not have the advertised effect, and some even make our health worse. Money dictates what scientists research, what courses college professors teach their students, and what sure-to-sell products industry should develop, to the detriment of products that cure and are most needed.

I don't wish to go on too much on this subject, but almost all the social and natural sciences are imposed by the collective ego.

In our era, anxiety and greed have produced an extremely unhappy, violent society that makes an enemy of itself and of its natural resources.

Most people live their lives like private dramas, so manipulated by their egos that their egos end up becoming their identities.

We are the result of our own disconnectedness. The ego dominates and conceals the present, hiding our true selves, our spiritual part. It keeps us from being alert and conscious of the present moment, conscious of the now. And because we are not evolving toward an ego-free consciousness, we are pushed toward self-destruction, directed by the envious mind which, at a universal level, has reached dangerous proportions.

There is a balance in the animal, mineral, and vegetable kingdoms. This balance is due to the fact that in each kingdom they consume only what they need to exist. But human nature is different. People are disposed to consume everything just to experience pleasure, even if it is not necessary for survival. This behavior disturbs the natural balance, which is constructed in levels, like a pyramid. When humans create an imbalance, nature itself begins to attack us. The first symptoms start at the inanimate level, such as climate phenomena, earthquakes, tsunamis, etc. Ecological issues are manifestations of four basic elements: fire, air, earth, and water. The fifth element is humanity.

What Are We Searching For?

Our task is to close the gap between our egoistic nature (receiving, consuming, and keeping for ourselves) and the influential nature (giving, contributing, sharing) which will give us the capacity to feel and act in harmony and in a bond with the Creator. The goal is to come to a balance between giving and receiving.

It is our deepest desire and primary interest to achieve a state of influence. With influence over our surroundings, we can alter the collision course now facing humanity, using our resources intelligently to achieve real social justice and true peace.

Once humanity has achieved our basic spiritual correction, we will be able to enjoy all the pleasures of the spiritual world—without fear of loss—as well as sensory and mundane pleasures; though these are not our goal except insofar as they are part of our spiritual objective.

What we want, what we seek, is to be connected, to have everything come together just right, to have life run like a Swiss watch, to be satisfied with what we have, even though we sometimes could use more money, and that everything we do should be the good of ourselves, but also for the good of others.

Helping and sharing the wisdom and understanding of our spirituality with others is like planting divine seeds in people's minds and hearts.

Now is the time for spiritual achievement.

The Daily Struggle

Our daily struggle is to find a way to live happy and content with every day and every moment of our lives, with everything we have, and what we lack.

This does not mean that we should accept situations that cause pain, suffering, or any other problem as they are and not do anything to change them.

First, we should try to understand what caused the problem to materialize in us. Our problem is that we do not understand the reason for things.

Why did I trip and scrape my knee? Why my left knee?

Imagine if we could understand the celestial reasons why things occur. Simply comprehending what happens to us would benefit us. Having a problem and understanding its cause is like healing a rift, or paying a debt. With this understanding, we are on a direct road to improvement, as much for physical or material problems as for our spiritual position.

Consciously accepting the situation, understanding it using our reason, and focusing on the present immediately leads us to accept it with positivity, and in that way, at the least, we can achieve a certain serenity.

This is not to deny the fact that when we act it consequently may create a new situation. We suffer from a spiritual lag, and as a result our true experience is hidden from us. We have to find our true self, the one we need to become to connect ourselves to the essence of the Creator, the divine soul within us, which we will explain in the next chapter.

We must carry on our daily struggle in peace and tranquility, whether we are working, with family and friends, studying or teaching, in any situation, expected or unexpected, by choice or obligation, sick or in the middle of a battle. Nothing is negative. Everything that happens to us happens for a reason, and that reason is always positive and always for our good. Whether we experience it in a positive way or we feel it as suffering and pain. Everything is positive.

It's appropriate to add here that reasonable optimism is a good quality, and very useful in life.

The important thing is to answer the question of whether we have tried hard enough and whether we have fought for spirituality in our lives. Have we truly wanted it? He who lives spiritually knows that life does not end with death.

Death is the end of the present illusion, the end of the body. The soul never dies.

We will explain later, and in full detail, the process of achieving tranquility and becoming content with what we have and what comes our way.

Spiritual Reality

Human beings are the highest creation on Earth. We differ from animals in our ability to speak and differentiate among each other. The purpose of creating man was to reveal the "divine image" within us. But this "divine image," which we commonly call a soul, only makes sense in interaction with others.

Spiritual reality is only revealed via a connection between two or more human beings under reciprocal conditions. A single person cannot achieve spirituality for him or herself without a relationship to another person. In contrast, two or more people can live the spiritual reality that is love, charity, hope, passion, courage, integrity, gratitude, justice, friendship, compassion, patience, tolerance, mercy, joy, responsibility, harmony, etc., in short, acts of kindness for and with another.

Practicing true spirituality will quickly lead us to the conclusion that serving people and connecting with others to help them is real happiness, and makes us feel whole and satisfied. Why not lend a hand to others? The world has supported, fed, and taught us everything, whether we deserved it or not. We could start by simply helping someone in need, teaching others a new skill, or sharing an honest, kind word with a passerby.

Any interpersonal relationship between two or more people has the potential to develop into a mutually-beneficial spiritual relationship—mutually beneficial both for the giver and the receiver—and this brings peace and well-being to any situation, favorable or detrimental, in which we find ourselves.

Spiritual DNA

Human genetic information is carried by DNA, the abbreviation for Deoxyribonucleic acid. DNA is responsible for the hereditary transmission of that information.

Similarly, we can say that every human being has spiritual DNA.

Spiritual DNA is the carrier of each individual's spiritual genetic information. Spiritual DNA is also responsible for the transmission and transcendence of that spiritual genetic information.

Every person's spiritual system is activated by their spiritual DNA. Spiritual DNA is what guides a person's existence.

This means that our spiritual goal is already inside us, "recorded" inside our own spiritual being.

If we understand and recognize our spiritual DNA, it will direct us toward a life of tranquility, fulfillment, richness, prosperity, joy, and mental peace.

The first thing we should do is to recognize the spiritual dimension inside ourselves as perfect. The spiritual dimension has the potential to turn us into influential beings, like the divine image we received. All this despite the fact that we are flesh and blood and have limitations. Our spiritual DNA comes inscribed with the codes of the attributes of the Creator.

Managing the Spiritual Project

As we mentioned earlier, a spiritual project can only be developed between two or more people. The minimal expression of a spiritual project includes two people: one who gives or influences, and another who receives. When I unite with one or many people, we construct a spiritual foundation together, and the dimensions of each person's spiritual projects and their benefits are exponentially increased.

A group, cohort, team, association, or congregation, etc. of people is the social medium where we can develop ourselves. Having a team is fundamental for spiritual growth.

Simply having the need to search for a spiritual world is enough in common for a community of connected people. A shared spiritual project gives us a unifying point or connecting bridge among all and between each of the participants in the project. Being joined in that way does not get in the way of having other points of unity in different projects. It is not a union that affects other unions.

Creating a group or groups around a spiritual project, no matter what it is, means building a team that will be successful in any project they take on. In addition to the positive results they will achieve, each individual's spirituality will grow and become stronger.

Spiritual relationships among various groups are fundamental for creating social networks oriented toward spiritual goals, and thereby gaining influence over society in general. How good it would be to have direct and immediate influence in society! Imagine the feeling of inner peace and glory that would come from living in complete harmony with our peers and with the environment.

But we can't forget that humans are products of the social environment in which they share ups and downs with their peers. We live "caged" by the society we live in. Whatever the society or group may be, good or bad, we are under its influence at all times. It is very difficult to escape this prison, and may be achieved only partially, and with great effort. Its influence surrounds us as much physically as socially, culturally, intellectually, and emotionally. The cultural invasion that we are victims of 24 hours a day (except for practicing Jews who keep the *shabat*, or day of rest, who suffer only six days) besieges our daily lives via TV, internet, radio, newspapers, cell phones, etcetera.

It's clear that if we are influenced by a group of people ruled only by their basic receiving nature, whether it be a small group or the entire society, we will continue to live in exile, a terrible reality.

From all this we can understand how important it is to have a spiritual team in the society we live in. The better it is, the greater will be our benefit, as we will be the result of something higher. A community with spiritual projects won't feel like a prison, but like being part of a composition in which we adjust to our daily lives with satisfaction and tranquility.

Later we will discuss in detail constitution, conditions, and other topics related to spiritual teams.

To begin to advance spiritually we need to create a propitious environment that encourages us and provides us with the basic, vital elements that will allow us to manifest the spiritual reality. This advantageous environment is a strong spiritual team of like-minded people in harmony with each other.

Chapter 2. The Creator

Although the purpose of this book is not to drown the reader in Kabbalistic knowledge about how the spiritual system works, it is still necessary to define and refine certain basic terms related to the composition of the soul according to the Kabbalah, which will help us later with our analysis and understanding of the spiritual system explained in the following chapters.

As we mentioned in the prologue, we will use appropriate words in our language in our definitions, but it's also important to include the original terms in Hebrew to make it easier for the reader to become familiar with them, research, and gain a deeper understanding from other sources. The words used in the definitions are simply labels for basic concepts, and therefore we shouldn't let ourselves be swayed by their names in our language, but rather focus on the concept behind them.

As we have said, man's natural tendencies are to receive, desire, enjoy, need, and consume, which are diametrically opposed to those of the Creator, to give, influence, and share.

The Creator's qualities, His essence, are latent within us. Our goal must be to find our own divine part and to become more like the essence of the Creator, overcoming our consumerist natures.

It is written that "there is no other apart from (the Creator). He is one, unique and immutable." This means that there is no other force on earth capable of acting against Him. In the *Bible* it is written, "God created man in His own image" (Genesis 1:27).

This being so, it is reasonable to ask: since the Creator is one and unique, and nothing exists outside of Him, why is each person distinct and different from others spiritually? The answer is that spirituality only makes sense when we are interacting with another person or a group of people. Everyone possesses certain spiritual characteristic which are more prominent than others. When I connect with someone, their spiritual DNA influences me and, in turn, my spiritual DNA influences them. This results in an "exchange" of the predominant characteristics of each, which creates a relationship between the spiritual DNA of the predominant parts of each individual as a mutual benefit. First example: if a person donates money to a needy family, both the giver and the receiver are satisfied and grateful to the other for participating, the one by receiving—thereby satisfying necessities—and the other by giving help. A second example: the author of a book wants to have an impact. The readers are influenced and will, in turn, impact the author. This is how a spiritual relationship works.

Every person expresses the Creator in their own way. The Creator shines in everyone in a different way.

Therefore we can conclude that a perfect state of true peace and tranquility between people can be described as a plurality of spiritual characteristics based on reciprocal conditions of mutual impact which exalt and overcome all differences.

The Creation Process: The Material and the Intangible.

It's not possible for us to know every detail of the Creator. We can only see his works and his actions.

The Creator made two realms: the spiritual and the material. In the Bible, it says that the Creator created Heaven (the spiritual, intangible part) and the Earth (the material part).

All the things around us –what we see, hear, feel, touch, and smell—have an equivalent representation in the spiritual world.

Not only that, but each thing begins as something spiritual, and later becomes physical. Everything that happens in this world, any decree or order that takes effect in our lives first has a spiritual expression that came before.

When we say that there is a spiritual world parallel to this one, we can't say how closely the physical world we perceive resembles the abstract spiritual form, nor how the spiritual world affects the physical.

We can't know why the Creator conceived Creation. But we can understand that the purpose of Creation is to give individuals the possibility of experiencing pleasure, to give them the ability to experience the feeling of well-being that comes with satisfying a desire; that is, to receive Spiritual Light (defined later).

Creation can be divided into four levels of reality: a) basic physical elements and primary materials; b) the real form of objects created based on physical materials; c) the abstract form of material objects, the spiritual aspect of things (this is the topic of the Zohar); and d) the spiritual essence of the

Creator, which is printed in our spiritual DNA, and hidden for now.

The Creator made both the spiritual part, called the Spiritual Light (provider) and the material aspect, called the Kli (receptor of the Light, as will be explained further on). These two parts are vital to Creation. When the Light influences someone, it comes directly to their entire being (body, intellect, and emotions), called Kli, bodily receptacle. The Spiritual Light is not tangible, nor can it be seen, but its properties are reflected in the Kli.

To better understand the process of Creation, we'll add a few facts that, without going into too much detail, are important.

There is a first step that precedes Creation, which we call the Infinite. The Infinite is where the Light and the Kli are together and blended, and where, despite being radically opposed, they mix together, without any distinction between them. The Light and Kli can't exist the one without the other.

The Light was created in the sense of "something that was created from something that already existed," while the Kli was created in the sense of "something that was created out of nothing" (*ex nihilo*).

Beginning from the Infinite, the Creator created or "conceived" Creation by separating those two opposites, the Light and the Kli.

Once they are separated in Creation, the Spiritual Light's role is to "expand," illuminate, or "dress" the Kli. Without the Kli, there is no way to receive the Light.

Now, in this state, the process of Creation is manifested when the Light begins to come to the Kli, not to the entire Kli, but rather to certain parts. There are certain "impediments," judgements or laws (*dinim*, in Hebrew) that don't allow the Kli, for the moment, to enjoy and receive the Light completely.

But it's impossible for the Kli to exist solely on the basis on judgements, laws, and edicts. With only the *dinim* the Kli breaks and can't sustain the Light that comes to it. We couldn't live in a world of only judgements and laws.

In Creation, in order for the Kli to be able to fully receive the Light, the Kli carries and creates within itself elements of mercy and compassion (*rachamim*, in Hebrew), in order to be able to neutralize and sweeten the judgements that occur in the Kli. When the laws are softened this way, the Light can reach all parts of the Kli without breaking it.

Once mercy and compassion are added to the existing laws, this is when our role begins in Creation, the work of correcting and improving our souls.

This is the current state of the Kli for every person in the world. Humans are only able to live thanks to the integration of a state of compassion with a state of judgement. Without compassion, there is no life.

Part of the purpose of this book is to be able to understand how the Light and the Kli interact.

We define these terms below.

Spiritual Light

Spiritual Light is an intangible force or energy that comes into a person, creates a new state of consciousness and increases their level of influence on people.

These new characteristics add an injection of wisdom, knowledge, intelligence, maturity, introspection, and greater clarity in all areas encompassed by this new state of illumination in daily life.

Spiritual Light is always present and is the only force in the universe we live in.

When the Light shines within the Kli, this is called a "soul." The soul can be subdivided into five parts or levels according the quality of its spiritual intensity, as will be explained further in a later chapter.

The Creator is absolute; there is no way to change or influence Him. Only the individual themselves can change.

Spiritual Light influences us at all times. It is infinite and has limitless power. Humans are not built to be able to receive the Light directly. Part of the Light is intercepted, obstructed. We may say it is "filtered" by levels and worlds between the Light and ourselves, intended to allow the Light to enter and spread selectively, according to our ability to respond to the Creator with the same intensity and thereby maintain a balance. There is a basic difference between traditional religion and the Kabbalah. In religious practice, one asks the Creator to personally intervene and change circumstances according to one's desires to improve the present reality. The study of the Kabbalah shows us that we ourselves are the only ones who can change our reality. Individuals who are conscious of their nature and condition as a receptor should convert themselves into giving people, who influence and share with others, like the Creator. Given that, and for the moment, it is difficult for us to find complete spirituality within ourselves, we say that the divine is "in exile."

As we mentioned earlier, the purpose for which humanity was created was to reveal our "divine image," the revelation of the Creator, whose essence is in our spiritual DNA. Everything is manifested through the Creator; nothing exists outside.

Hidden Spiritual Forces

When wisdom, or the illumination of the Light within us, doesn't have a material representation, in other words it doesn't have "clothing" and cannot be measured, we say that it is hidden.

We can only understand the Creator through our similarity to his essence. The essence of the Creator is revealed within us every time we make spiritual progress. The Creator becomes more and more visible in us.

The Light needs material to be expressed. Like electricity is manifested through a cable or capacitor, the Light is manifested through the Kli. And, like electricity, it can only be measured when it encounters an opposing force or resistance.

Spiritual Light is composed of five parts or levels, which we will explain more later.

The Light can be manifest and clear to a person, like it is in nature, but it can also be hidden. This means the Light isn't represented or "clothed" in any material form, and therefore can't be measured.

Hidden Light appears in two ways: simple concealment and double concealment.

Simple Concealment

This is when we are aware that—for the moment—we don't have the right tools or the correct, refined qualities to perceive the Creator. We aren't disconnected, but rather opposed to the Creator. The solution is to nullify our own egos to allow the divine gene we possess to shine.

We say that simple concealment is seeing the Creator's back because we are very close to Him (albeit behind Him), and it's possible to see that something has happened to us or something isn't working, for example, when we're not happy or nothing comes out like we hope. But we don't suffer, we can manage our discontent by understanding that this is what the Creator has decreed for now, and that it shouldn't be interpreted as punishment but rather put in context, without exaggerating it, but without forgetting it. We haven't lost faith.

Double Concealment

Double concealment is when we don't even notice the presence of the Creator near us and we aren't remotely conscious of any connection with Him, so much so that we don't even feel we are opposed to Him. We can't feel that we have something of the Creator in ourselves. We feel abandoned by Him. We accept our suffering (or our pleasure) as part of our fate; we have no faith. Double concealment is also called concealment within the concealed.

People who are different from us, who are successful, in good health, who seem self-assured, aren't interested in or conscious of the spiritual system in their lives at all are an example of double concealment. There are some who have become very wealthy in unsavory ways and who think that we, who aspire to be like the Creator, are poor, sick, stupid, or primitive.

Kli (Recipient, Spiritual Bodily Receptor)

The Kli—a Hebrew word which means recipient, vessel, or bodily receptor—is a desire within me that is ready to be corrected, that is, prepared to receive Spiritual Light.

A person's Kli is their spiritual receptor or storage place for the Spiritual Light.

As we've discussed, the Infinite is the state before the Creation, in which the Creator kept the Light and the Kli in a state of perfect union despite their opposing natures. While together, united, the Kli perceived that the power of infinite influence it enjoyed at the time was due entirely to the fact of being joined to the Light, and was not due to itself or its own merits.

Then the Kli decided that it didn't want to have influence this way. The Kli didn't want to continue to receive the Light for free, without effort or sweat, as it was in the Infinite. The Kli began to develop and experience shame (*bushá*, in Hebrew), which is the feeling of loss of dignity caused by receiving the Light without effort, without work, that is, without earning it.

This is when the Light and the Kli separated. The Kli left the Light. Now that they are separate, it is up to us, the individuals, to fill the Kli once again with Spiritual Light, but this time in a deserving way, without shame.

So our task is to refine our Kli. It is imperfect, so we must correct and polish it in order to attain the maximum possible Spiritual Light.

The Kli is divided according to its "density" or "refinement," and in these states will receive the five levels or intensities of Spiritual Light corresponding to the Kli's levels of refinement.

The Spiritual Light's levels of intensity are located within the Kli in ten different areas called *sefirot* according to the Light's density, which will be explained further on. We can say that the Light "clothes" the Kli with different "clothes."

The bigger the Kli, the more Spiritual Light can enter, and thereby increase the person's power and influence because then their soul is closer to the Creator and more like Him.

When the Spiritual Light enters the Kli, one experiences an "ascent" (in Hebrew, *aliá*) or "rise", which means that the person's Kli has become larger and there is more space for Spiritual Light to enter.

We can also talk about the Kli of a group of people. When a group of people works together on any type of spiritual project, be it studying, praying, meditating, or working at a non-profit or for charity, each person's Kli is added to the rest of the *Kelim* (plural of Kli), forming the group's Kli. Where mutual guarantee (explained further on) exists among the members of a group, whether physically present or not, that union has a group Kli. There's no limit to the number of people who can join a group's Kli; they can reach the millions. The group of people can even be virtual (communicating by phone, apps, internet, or any other network).

We can also talk about the universal Kli, which is the Kli of all people on Earth. But, for now –unfortunately—we are still in spiritual exile. Being in spiritual exile is a sign that we do not have the ability to fill the universal collective Kli.

Israel (*Yashar-El*: Direct to the Creator)

A person who works for a spiritual life is called "Israel."

In Hebrew, the word "Israel" is composed of two parts: "Isra-El" or "*yashar-El*", which means to direct oneself "directly to the Creator." Today there is a great gap between the majority of humanity and the Creator.

In Gematria (a science in which each Hebrew letter and word has a numerical value and meaning), the words "nature" (in Hebrew *teva*) and "creator" (in Hebrew, *boreh*) have the same numerical value. Similarly, boreh is a Hebrew word composed of two words: *bo*, which means come, and *reh*, to look. In other words, "come and look." I came, and I also attained something. The goal is to achieve equivalence of form with the essence of the Creator.

When the Spiritual Light comes to what is concealed, it "illuminates" us. What was hidden is made visible. We can see it, measure it, and quantify it.

As we discussed, we call a person Israel who is on a direct line pointing "directly to the Creator," as expressed through the way they live and their spiritual relationships with others.

Every person is at a given spiritual point or location. The spiritual goal is to arrive at the point or setting where we will find the Creator, source of Spiritual Light.

Time Doesn't Exist

How long does humanity need to come out of exile and reach a state of perpetual revealed Light?

The Kabbalah explains that the term "time" doesn't exist in spirituality. Here we'll try to explain this abstract concept.

We refer to the "distance" between the point we are at currently in our spiritual development and the point where the Creator is as "time."

We can visualize this geometrically (see Figure 1, below). A straight central vertical path (cylinder): The Creator. Each individual (marked il1, il2, up to il7) who is advancing directly to the Creator is called "Israel." We can recognize as a "distance" (marked d1, d2, up to d7) the space between where we are spiritually and where we should be, the Creator. Eventually, at the end of our spiritual correction, we join the central line. This means we have reached the same spiritual level as the essence of the Creator, the end of the

correction of our soul, where there is a balance or
equivalence of form, a concept that will be explained further.

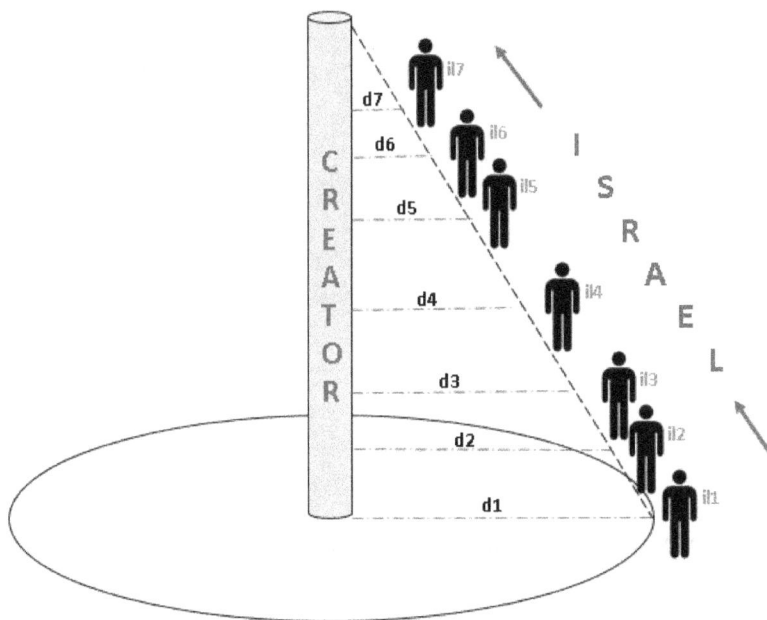

Time Doesn't Exist

Figure 1

Therefore, time does not exist. It is an illusion, because we may achieve the Creator's characteristics of influence at any time, and immediately join the vertical line. Still being unprepared to openly and continually influence those around us is what creates the impression of "time." It is the "time" left for us to act and to come to our full power of influence like the Creator. But as we already mentioned, neither time nor space exists, we can reach a balance of spiritual forces at any time.

The convergence point is when the dualities join together, becoming a single different, all-powerful entity. For example, happiness and unhappiness are actually one, and will join in the end into a single point. We only see the illusion of time that separates us, that is, the "time" that delays us in going from being unsatisfied to being satisfied, or the "distance" that separates unhappiness from happiness.

Shabat

Shabat (Sabbath or Saturday) is the seventh day of Creation, the seventh day of the week in Judaism.

Shabat isn't required for the spiritual system described in this book to work. But for Jewish readers, keeping *shabat* is one of the most efficient ways to advance spiritually.

There are many ways to advance spiritually. In this book, we describe a spiritual system that is relevant for everyone, regardless of religion, credo, race, color, or gender.

The topic of *shabat* would fill several books, so we will only briefly mention the spiritual, rather than religious, significance of this day of abundant spiritual energy.

The Hebrew word *shabat* means "stop," "cease to do," "pause." It is sometimes translated as "rest" due to the conditions that practicing Jews must follow in order to receive the spiritual energies present on this day.

Keeping or observing *shabat* brings positive spiritual results during the week, which begins on Sunday and ends six days later, the following Saturday. These spiritual results will be manifested in all our daily tasks, which means a spiritual advance for the person, evident in all areas.

In the first six days of Creation, the Creator created the spiritual forms out of nothing (*ex nihilo*)—which is the Kli— and on the seventh, the Creator continued to create new spiritual things out of spiritual things that already existed—the Light—which dresses the Kli.

Every day of the week contains the spiritual force with which we can connect to the Light. But *shabat*, for Judaism, is the only day when the Spiritual Light is present in a much more abundant, higher-quality, and more refined way, compared to the rest of the first six days of the week.

On this special day, the Light is in reach only for a person who observes and keeps *shabat*, which means that the person restricts the vast majority of their tasks and daily routines. These are avoided almost entirely, for the purpose of reaching the minimum conditions to be receptors of Spiritual Light.

On this day work is also voluntarily put on hold for 24 hours, the employer-employee relationship is paused and its effect nullified. Pollution is suspended and exploitation of people and animals is barred, every individual is free, and, in turn, must liberate all those who are subordinate to them. The goal is to create a physical environment of natural peace and universal balance, so that everything continues on its own momentum and inertia, without changes or disturbances at the mineral, vegetable, animal, or human level, so that the status quo of physical tranquility allows us to distinguish and capture the spiritual abundance that is present on Earth on this day without colliding with anything or anyone.

When I talk to people of my religion who still don't keep *shabat*, I explain to them that if they don't follow these conditions completely, they create interference between themselves and the spiritual charge, which interrupts this potent spiritual environment. For example: if we put a magnifying glass between the sun and a sheet of paper, after concentrating the ray of light for a few moments the heat generated by the light will burn a hole in the paper. But if we don't concentrate the ray of light we can't pierce the paper. Spiritually, *shabat* is the same: if we concentrate our efforts and activities into their minimal expression, we can penetrate and achieve a state of spiritual abundance simply by staying "restricted" from physical work and in peace with nature. In contrast, if we don't maintain this *status quo* of physical tranquility, we won't capitalize on the spiritual abundance, wasting the opportunity to advance spiritually.

On this day of the week, a person is disconnected from the mundane and the physical, and has an opportunity to elevate their level of spirituality. For this reason we customarily call it the "Day of Rest".

Shabat is one of the sources of spiritual energy with which we start the week and live the rest of it with an eye toward the following *shabat* to recharge ourselves again. In summary: liberty and order for the person and their soul.

Prayer and Meditation

Mediation and prayer are preparation and a way of drawing close to spiritual reality. These practices are essentially methods to achieve a state of consciousness and true presence with more clarity, peace, and mental tranquility.

It's worth adding that these practices—both meditation and prayer—should be engaged in for the purpose of improving one's ability to have a positive influence on others. If these activities are used only to benefit the person's internal peace, without connection to any benefit for others, they can't be connected to spirituality per se, they are only another facet of ego. When a person effectively practices prayer or meditation with another person or group of people with the goal of doing spiritual work that is when the power of influence among them may be revealed.

With respect to prayer, I'm personally adept at it, preferably with a group. For example, when ten or more men pray together, they generate a much larger Kli than simply the "sum" of the Kelim of all present. Each participant receives Spiritual light within the group Kli which is much larger than their own Kli, resulting in a net advantage in that person's spiritual growth.

When we pray, we chant hymns, we pronounce words of praise for the Creator and His Creation, we strengthen our spiritual growth and the image of divinity within ourselves. Praying the same text together accelerates the spiritual growth of the community.

Acts of Kindness (*mitzvot*) and Behavior Norms

The most direct way to live a spiritual reality is to carry out acts of kindness (*mitzvot*, in Hebrew) or to conduct ourselves correctly, with honor, decorum, and respect for others in everything we do in our daily lives.

A *mitzvá* (singular of *mitzvot*) is a correction of our desires. For example, if we give bread to a hungry person, we effect a spiritual renewal, a soul correction that represents one more brick in the construction of universal peace, a bridge of spiritual connection between two or more people, regardless of who is the giver and who is the receiver.

The only purpose of spirituality is to participate in every moment, unified with Creation. Acts of kindness towards others make us part of the whole of Creation itself. We can have an impact, including on its very essence.

If, on the other hand, we don't do acts of kindness, there is no point at all to spirituality. We will not become part of Creation, but will be relegated to living in this world as a mere consequence, without any power to modify or influence anyone or anything.

Revelation

When spiritual force comes to us, we experience a "lift," which we call a revelation.

A revelation is a manifestation of the force or Spiritual Light that comes to a person after having been hidden. Through revelation the person's faith in the Creator and in them self is strengthened. The person then brings this internal force from the revelation to the texts, to their studies, and to their teacher or guide to be corrected by them for a better understanding of the world we live in.

The Creator is revealed to all created beings according to each being's desires. Revelation is manifested when a person feels the Creator's kindness, peace, and constant satisfaction. For example, when we earn enough money without too much effort, when we have no problems and suffer no pains, when we are respected, loved, and successful. If someone wants something, they ask for it and receive it; the Light shines inside them: the person is king. With each new act we become more successful and achieve more positive spiritual revelations.

On the other hand, the more egotistical we are and the fewer good deeds we do, the more our spiritual success will be compromised. In other words, as we diminish our positive spiritual expressions the negative spiritual expressions in our lives increase.

Chapter 3. Terms and Definitions

The following are definitions of basic concepts necessary to understand the spiritual model described in this book.

Reshimó: Spiritual DNA

As explained in the previous chapter, the Light and Kli were together in the Infinite. To conceive Creation, the Light and Kli separated so that when our correction is complete the Light can return to fill the Kli completely, this time in a deserving way, without shame.

Once the Kli was separated from and empty of the Light, all that remained inside was a "spiritual genetic imprint" of the Light. This imprint of the Spiritual Light was recorded on the Kli when it was joined with the Light in the Infinite. This imprint is called *reshimó*, and we can think of it as the DNA in an individual's spiritual system.

The spiritual DNA or *reshimó* contains an inheritance of spiritual "genes" from Creation, combined with the spiritual journey of the soul so far. These spiritual genes define our desires, needs, and the entire spiritual topography of our Kli, including the divine part that comes from the Creator.

Every characteristic of our personalities is recorded within our vast spiritual DNA, both those we acquire and those we inherit.

Desire

Man's spiritual system is composed solely of desires, planted within us by the Creator. Desire is the very material from which we were created. Our flesh and blood beings define our receiving, desiring, and needy natures. It is impossible to reveal truth and reality because everything occurs within our desire. This means that every image we see, our movements, space, time, and even volume are perceptions of our desire.

The goal is to be able to control our desires. When we cannot control the power of our own desires, we experience the true sensations of the outside world, which are manipulated by ego.

Desire's expectations determine our perception and consciousness. What the heart wants, the mind perceives. Sometimes when we have a certain craving, as we drive through the city our senses are tempted by places we could satisfy it.

But if we could control our desires, restricting them, accepting the present as it is, surrendering to the present moment unconditionally, we would see clearly that the world is internal, that everything is inside us and that we can change this desire, because by neutralizing our ego we will clearly see it is for our own good, the good of others, and the good of the community.

One desire is presented to us as a function of time, another gives us a sense of change, and other a sense of volume. Colors, sounds, smells, flavors, measurements and physical contact are all different desires which, together, represent the world for us, the material world that surrounds us.

By correcting a desire, one moves closer to the Creator. When we are able to correct all our desires so that they all join inside us as one "scaffold," then we will discover that the whole universe is inside us and nothing takes place or exists outside of what we are. As we said earlier, we live within our desires, given that they are the only thing the Creator implanted in us.

Everything is centered on our desires, which are, in turn, a reflection of our ego. The day we understand our true desires in relation to others we will begin to reveal the spiritual part in each person. People must yield themselves and control their egos, but without interpreting this as a sign of weakness, but rather as a convenient personal improvement.

Later, in the section covering the elements of the spiritual model, we will get into the details of the fields or spheres of our desires, or in other words, how we perceive our world.

Our task as people is to discern which parts of our desires we should correct with the clear intention of having an impact and giving to people. We should also be discerning about which parts of ourselves haven't yet been corrected, limiting ourselves in that desire. What can be corrected will define the amount of Spiritual Light a person has and the size of a person's Kli.

Rabbi Najman of Breslov, a teacher and sage at the end of the 18th Century and beginning of the 19th, wrote in his *Collected Teachings* (*Likutey Moharán* in Hebrew) that people often have unsatisfied desires because they do not have a sufficiently large Kli to receive abundance. This author says that a person, by simply articulating his desires, brings them closer to reality, or in other words, the person's own desire helps to build and expand their Kli.

The Law of Equivalence of Form or Law of Spiritual Balance

The Law of Equivalence of Form—or Law of Spiritual Balance—says that those who share similar spiritual properties attract one another according to how similar they are. When the similarity is complete, they join in perfect harmony.

We have already seen that the Creator is an absolute and unchanging force. The more similar a person's spiritual life is to the Creator's characteristics, the more power to influence they will have. Conversely, the more different they are, the less influence they will receive. The Law of Equivalence of Form is the basis of the whole spiritual process: the closer we are to being like the Spiritual Light, the more influential we are.

The Law of Equivalence of Form works from the Creator toward us and from us toward the Creator, which is why it is also called the law of Spiritual Balance. Proportional to the amount of Light we receive from the Creator, we can link to Him and "influence" like Him with the same force, but our influence is directed at others. This maintains a balance.

Additionally, the individual may feel it necessary to "respond" to the Creator by bringing Him happiness (*nájat rúaj* in Hebrew), pleasure, and pride, just like a son makes his father happy when he sees him advance and triumph.

However, it's worth noting that the Creator doesn't need anything from anyone, much less from us; the Creator only gives, He does not receive. We can't "respond" to him per se. What we can and should do is work to improve our value in our relationships with others and perfect our spiritual projects in order to achieve a closer equivalence of form.

We mentioned earlier that we cannot free ourselves from our nature. We have a need to receive, to enjoy ourselves, and we are constantly questioning whether we are happy, if we want something else, if we could enjoy ourselves more or improve our position. But according to the Law of Equivalence, we must achieve a state equivalent to the Creator's, although it is the opposite of our consumerist nature. We say it is opposite because we must always be checking and asking ourselves how to benefit others more and more and how to give from ourselves to benefit others.

So, how can we make this radical change?

Within our spiritual DNA there is a "gene," a spiritual spark, which we call the "the point in the heart" and which has the minimum basic properties of the Creator: those of giving and sharing with others.

"The Point in the Heart" (Desire for Spirituality)

This is the spiritual segment or "gene" which has the minimum properties of the Creator. It is the starting point from which a person's spiritual part to begins to try to reach the Spiritual Light. We call people whose "points in the hearts" are already active "Israel," as we mentioned earlier.

This "gene" is active in people with an active spiritual inclination and those who are already started on the path of understanding and using their spiritual systems. This "gene" is currently inactive in most people.

Once it is activated, life will never be the same. The "Point in the heart" will guide a person to spiritual maturity and will be the beginning of an awakening that will stimulate internal changes. The person begins to perceive the world with a sense of consciousness of the now, and begins to enter a world of peace, satisfaction, love, and happiness with what they do and have.

The "point in the heart" makes it possible to distance oneself from the desire to receive pleasure purely through the ego. In accommodating the ego, the person should analyze it and control it from the outside, looking at exactly what the Creator has built. This ability to see what the Creator has built is called "faith," which is higher than reason. Studying the "point in the heart" lets us see how Creation Works.

The vast majority of people in society focus on bettering their lives socioeconomically. Only a small number recognize their "points in the heart," and awaken the beginnings of their spiritual selves. The true purpose of life is the revelation of a higher world.

But even having an activated "point in the heart" isn't enough to draw the Creator's properties within us. We must draw the Spiritual Light to ourselves. But how? This depends on how much we resemble the Creator. And how can we become more like Him? By creating a partnership or joining a group of people who already have active "points in the heart" like ours.

This will be the topic of later chapters that will explain ways to do so.

Perception of Reality

Our perception of the world is completely based on our five senses, and as we know, they are limited. We can't know what is beyond our senses.

The way we conceive of the Creator depends entirely on our own ability to capture reality. We must start by acknowledging that what we perceive isn't what is happening around us, but rather the sum of all the internal reactions accumulated from our experiences, etched inside us. We recognize matter and its forms, but we can't perceive the true essence of things nor their abstract forms.

Nothing exists outside the human mind. Each person is conscious of their existence, even the fact of reading this page now, for example. We are unique in our consciousness, we never forget about ourselves. All our feelings and experiences are inside us. What we see through the window comes from ourselves. We see a tree, for example, which is outside of us, but let there be no doubt: our body, the window, and the tree are within our consciousness, inside us. The only true limits to what we can be, have, or do are self-imposed. Those limits do not exist outside ourselves. The reason we can't walk through walls is because we are controlled by the same rules we have created through and with the help of our senses.

Our senses are a reflection of our state of consciousness. It's impossible to perceive our spiritual selves because our senses are what determine the development of our ego. We don't know how to adjust our senses to receive the Light of spiritual reality, because we don't know what to receive, we don't know what the subject is. Even at the physical, bodily level, there are researchers and scientists who confirm that a person can't perceive any external stimulus if it hasn't already been defined within them.

What would happen if we had the ability to clearly perceive abstract forms and the essence of things? Or, better put, what if the image of the Creator was clear?

If we had the revealed Light within ourselves without having worked to achieve it, it would make us feel a loss of dignity, because if we were to see the spiritual essence invested in each thing and in every detail we see and do, we wouldn't be motivated to study, progress, and become more like the Creator. We have spiritual DNA from the essence of the

Creator and His characteristics are inside us although they haven't been revealed by our senses. We must discover them by studying the spiritual system; we won't get anywhere using our senses alone.

To have the "divine image" of the Creator's essence revealed in all we are, first we must learn the forms that are opposed to the Creator, then we can begin to build qualities like the Creator's. Once the opposing forms are known, the way to activate the DNA of the divinity latent inside us will be clear.

Similar to the way our senses can perceive our physical surroundings, our Kli can understand the spiritual reality that belongs to each of us. The Kli can't know about exterior reality, it only understands the reality within itself. We can think of the Kli as a sixth sense, which has the drive to acquire the Creator's characteristics.

Usually, we call the perception of the reality within the Kli in its present static form being in "this world" or "the current world." And being in a "next world" or "higher world" is the perception of reality within the Kli when it beings to "accumulate" spiritual energy, to have influence, and continue working to become fully like the Creator's essence.

The process of our Kli adapting, adjusting, and growing is a life's work, until the correction is complete.

The Soul

Generally, we call the spiritual part of the person, the energy, force, or desire directed to spirituality, "soul."

An individual's soul is called "spiritual matter," and an individual's real desires are the forms that "dress" the spiritual matter, which is that individual's "current world."

A person can reach the state of the Creator's essence by understanding how his spiritual DNA is put together, which is to say, his desires. Once the desires are exposed and the person is conscious of them, the person can transform them, refine them, and correct them until they rise to the level of love and influence.

In the next chapter we will explain the levels of the soul.

Living in Our Present

What is the present?

According to the dictionary, the present is what is in front of or in the presence of someone, the instant in which it happens, the current moment, the now.

However, some people define the present as this instant, or the fine line joining the past and future, in other words, as something that doesn't exist.

Without going too deep into a discussion of form, but getting into some depth, we recognize the present as something broader than simply the line joining past and future, something related to the now, our life right at this moment, in the era we live in.

We must live considering the present the only thing we have now; the past can't be relived, it is already dead, and the future hasn't come yet. The past and the future don't exist, only memories or promises.

One important question for managing spirituality is: what do the past and the future have to do with the present?

The answer is simply that the experiences of the past and those of the future are products of our ego, because, as we've said before, desires can present as a function of time.

The topic of living in the present and being immune to the past and the future has been well covered and explained in detail in *The Power of Now* by Eckhart Tolle. I will cite a few of his ideas, which can also support us in understanding the spiritual model discussed here.

Immunity to the Past and Future

We must live in our present and be immune to the fantasies that stem from the past or the future.

In general, people live the present with thoughts, feelings, emotions, or traces of the past. And we can ask ourselves, what do these experiences have to do with a person's ego?

The answer is simple: a person's ego shines in the present compared a past experience or feeling which can influence us so much that it keeps us from having the chance to truly and objectively evaluate the present. The ego feeds on comparison to past experiences.

If we "neutralize" our egos to an extent that allows us to awaken and/or acquire characteristics of the Creator in ourselves, we will be able to live in the present consciously, peaceful and happy with whatever the moment brings.

For example, if someone did something and felt sadness, frustration, or fear, as a result, the person will compare that experience with what could happen if they do the same activity in the present. Obviously, between fear and not-fear, a person will choose not-fear every time. Choosing not-fear is simply focusing on the past to avoid it, without paying attention to the present and the current facts to choose freely, independent of the fear felt the first time. Present activity is conditioned by the fear of repeating unpleasant past experiences.

The opposite is also true. If a person experienced happiness or security, the person compares that experience with what might happen again, without taking into account that current conditions may be different.

We should be clear that the past itself isn't a negative thing. On the contrary, the past gives us important historical facts, information fundamental to understanding the present and planning the future. However, this information should be observed and analyzed dispassionately. As we know, those who don't understand the past are condemned to repeat it. The past provides extra information to help process present facts and thereby resolve situations in the best possible way.

Living constantly thinking of the future or the past keeps us from being here, in the present, from being conscious of the unique reality we have, from being able to live happy and satisfied with what we have.

We must live like artists: creating in our souls, without thoughts, without time or mind, but in peace and serenity.

Unfortunately many people spend years waiting for a better future or stuck in a motionless past.

Emotional Intelligence

According to Wikipedia, emotional intelligence is what allows us to be aware of our emotions and understand our feelings correctly.

To live in the present and be immune to the past and the future, we must have adequate emotional intelligence. If we make decisions "in cold blood," analyzing the pros and cons clearly, we will obtain better results. Being conscious of the moment, without thoughts anchored in the past or the future helps us to analyze the different possibilities in order to be able to apply the correct solutions.

Blame, regrets, resentments, complaints, sadness, bitterness, shame, affection, pity... are all feelings caused by thinking of the past causes that generated them. Sometimes we are disgusted by someone who has done us wrong; in these cases forgiveness in the present is much more important than past forgiveness, because it means internalizing it in the full consciousness of the moment. This emotional maturity or intelligence helps us to begin developing the characteristics needed to establish a spiritual system with little interference.

Emotions are mental reactions. We must learn to observe our emotions and thoughts to avoid being controlled by them. Emotion is a pattern of thoughts charged with energy and with the power to control us, displacing our consciousness of the present and making us lose our tranquil contemplation of the now. Emotion opens the doors to invading thoughts carrying long-extinct past occurrences or illusory futures.

Sometimes, even life seems senseless. We all go through times when depression taints life's meaning; our mind collapses and senselessness takes over. We can call this madness or unconsciousness.

Over time, many people turn negative due to the accumulation of psychological experiences. When a new opportunity comes in the present, they don't fully enjoy the situation because, sadly, they put up a certain, possibly baseless, resistance.

The same thing happens with the future. A person worried or distracted by the result of a decision which they won't know for a few days is letting their ego take control of their mind, leaving them without space to live in the present. The present should remain free of a future which hasn't yet happened because they will know the answer in a few days, there is no way to know it earlier. This doesn't preclude planning, making decisions, or taking action to prevent possible future situations. Indeed, it is advisable and necessary to plan future actions based on present facts.

Feelings of fear, uneasiness, anxiety, tension, stress, or worry are caused by thinking about the future, denying the present, which is the only thing that truly exists. For example, if we're invited to think that the future will be better, ideas like "my boss promised me that next year I'll get a raise" should be analyzed in the serenity of the now, because they are events that haven't happened yet. Boasting or feeling good about an activity still to come is to roundly deny the present and take refuge in an uncertain future. Emotional intelligence is an indispensable requirement for evaluating a promise. It's possible that the future will come together, but no claim about the future can be true now. It may happen, it may not. There's no way to know.

Chapter 4. The Spiritual System

How to reveal a system that can't be measured or perceive by any of our senses?

How can I start to share my energy, my talent, and my being with others now? How can I help?

There's a disconnection in each of us between our divine potential—the Creator's essence—and our current situation. It's like a veil covering the true source of Light, which isn't expressed, but which truly exists in our current world. The Light which isn't yet manifested is the source of human consciousness. What is hidden and not manifested are our absent senses.

People in whom the seed of spirituality, the "point in the heart," has been planted have a constant need to search. They need to find a system that allows access to spiritual truth at all levels and at all times.

Every vicissitude of life, each thing we see or encounter in our path tells us something. For example, as we walk, suddenly we may witness an unusual event, or something may happen that catches our attention: a car accident, a conversation between two people, a natural phenomenon, etc. In everything that happens in our lives, something belongs to us, directly or indirectly, something is talking to our consciousness, to our being, to our self; something is being taught to us and has the potential to make some spiritual part of ourselves to evolve.

Everything that happens to people, everything they are born with, everything they acquire throughout their lives, is for their good and is perfectly acceptable to their soul and body. A person's soul is eternal, because it is part of the universal soul that comes from the Creator, like every soul in the world. It's said that humanity's universal soul is Adam's soul. He was the first man endowed with the Creator's divine image in his spiritual DNA, called the "universal soul."

Every soul maintains a direct and special relationship with the Creator. When a person is born, the essential characteristics, like a spiritual map, are "recorded" in their spiritual genes, which will help them to choose the spiritual path they should follow to be able to refine and improve their soul in this world. That soul knows which parts of the spiritual DNA will need to be changed to achieve its greatest splendor.

With the spiritual requirements engraved on our spiritual DNA as a base, we can explain in plain language that the soul has a "discussion" with the Creator to "choose" and decide every detail, both physical and social, of our lives. They are the details that will help us to do our spiritual improvement during life. For example: the date and era of our birth, the place, who will be our parents, who our partner and our siblings will be, the day of our death, and so on.

For example, if someone is born with a physical abnormality such as blindness or paralysis, their soul is "in agreement and complete acceptance" that what they have is correct to improve their soul. There are spiritual reasons for each and every act that marks us, both those we consider "positive" and those that we consider "negative," everything that comes our way.

Everything that happens to us, "positive" or "negative," is for the good of our soul. Whether we are directly involved in what happens or as spectators, by our choice or by a major force that imposed on us, everything is good and for our good.

Sometimes it is very hard to understand that something that looks and feels "negative," something that happens that depresses us or puts us in a bad mood—a harsh blow, unbearable pain, a death, illness, economic loss, etc.—is positive and that its consequences are for our own good, for the improvement of our soul and its relationship with others.

As an example, if we try to explain the premature death of a young person, perhaps we'll never understand the reason. It's possible to put forward several ideas, but we'll mention just two, in general terms: 1) the young person's soul came to this world to finish something that was still necessary to complete their correction and finally purify their soul. 2) the pain that the young person's death causes their loved ones will help them to purify themselves and reflect on the Creator. Through the pain something unfinished will be corrected, like paying a spiritual "debt" and finishing a cycle of their soul.

Sometimes the immediate short-term analysis of a "negative" event is incomprehensible, and it is our duty to look for the good or positive reason why it happened. Negativity is simply our resistance to accepting the present as it is, due to not understanding that there is a "net gain" for us in everything that happens to us or which we witness.

Although it's not the topic of this book, we can mention briefly that the reasons an event or accident happened to us are connected to different spiritual variants, such as earlier lives of the same soul –reincarnation– which manifested in their time without the desired results, but are now re-lived, overcome, and corrected for the benefit and correction of our soul. The issue of souls reincarnating to rectify wrongs committed or missed spiritual opportunities in earlier lives is also a topic for another book.

When we are connected to our spiritual system, we begin to glimpse the forces that move things, the reasons, the whys, the goals and details of everything we are conscious or unconscious of, that is, everything that moves or exists in our lives.

Binary Spiritual Relationships

The spiritual model presented in this book is based on the spiritual relationship between two or more people, known as a "binary relationship." Each binary spiritual relationship has special meaning.

Every personal relationship can be interpreted as a binary relationship. For example: parent-child, husband-wife, etc.

When three people are spiritually associated (for example **A**lbert, **B**ob, and **C**arlos) there are three simple binary relationships: A-B, B-C, and A-C. These three relationships can also participate in other binary relationships, composed of A-BC, for example, or C-AB. For math lovers, we can say the number of possible binary relationships among x number of people is called N factorial (written N!). The factorial number is obtained by multiplying every number from one to N: 1 x 2 x 3 x 4 x 5 x 6 x7... x N = N! (Example: 2! = 1 x 2; 3! = 1 x 2 x 3 = 6; 4! = 1 x 2 x 3 x 4 = 24, etc.)

Spiritual Partner

A spiritual partnership is an example of a binary relationship between two people: husband and wife, two close friends, etc. Here we will refer to them as the masculine part and the feminine part.

Every one of us, both men and women, has a masculine spiritual aspect and a feminine spiritual aspect. In the spiritual system, the feminine aspect is the "receptive" part, and the masculine aspect is the "giving" part, the influential part.

A husband should see his feminine aspect reflected in his wife. She is the expression of his feminine aspect, that is, the receptive part of the man. The woman, in turn, sees the man as the masculine aspect within her, the part that gives and influences. Men and women exist for mutual service and complement each other, in the terms dictated by each individual's spiritual DNA.

In marriage, each partner should be committed to giving themselves completely and unconditionally to the other, with honesty and sincerity. The marital bond is essentially spiritual, governed by the spiritual merging of each member's Kli. The union of marriage unites two halves in one single soul: the partnership's Kli.

If the union is merely physical or material, it won't work. Although the relationship may continue, they will not enjoy it.

Interpersonal relations in couples such as husband-wife, boyfriend-girlfriend, parent-child, mother-baby, siblings, teacher-student, etc. are a topic for another time.

Women and Pregnancy

We would briefly like to mention the important spiritual relationship that exists between a mother and her unborn child.

Pregnancy is seen as a state of purification and connection of the baby's soul. It corresponds to the trials and tribulations that the souls of the baby and the mother must undergo before birth.

From the moment of fertilization, a direct spiritual relationship exists between the fetus and the mother's soul. It's worth mentioning that the father's soul is also directly related to the baby while it is inside the mother's womb. The baby's body develops under the directions of their own *reshimó* (spiritual gene) already "placed" in the unborn child, until the soul can be manifested, at a basic level, after approximately the first 20 weeks of pregnancy. This can vary from woman to woman, but there are some cases, depending on the mother's level of spirituality, in which the soul can manifest much earlier, even at the moment of conception.

As we've mentioned in earlier chapters, everything begins in the spiritual world, and later is manifested in the physical world. But what interests us here is what happens to this spiritual relationship once the woman already has the fetus in her womb, months before birth.

It is a powerful, special binary spiritual relationship, despite the fact that physically it is characterized by the fact that the two parties can't communicate verbally, by smell, or visually.

During pregnancy, there is a constant dialogue between the souls of the mother and those of the child or children. This spiritual connection has direct effects on the baby's physical development and, obviously, also on the mother's body, including her physical, emotional, intellectual, and psychological behavior. The spiritual connection between mother and child is so strong that, as we know, there can be changes in health in both the mother and fetus due to spiritual links between the two souls. For example, for the mother, nausea and vomiting can be interpreted as rejection manifested by her body due to a lack of harmony because the mother's soul hasn't yet linked completely to the child's, or vice versa.

My personal experience has shown me that just being aware of this spiritual reality, that there are two souls in constant connection, was important and had positive effects on my wife's pregnancy. Therapy and conversations I had with her during her pregnancy resulted in an excellent pregnancy, with normal anxiety, during which she never vomited once, and the total weight gain at the end of nine months was just 6 kilos, very acceptable for a woman who is 1.75m tall and weighs 60 kilograms. The delivery was brief and without complications. The talks about the binary spiritual relationship between my wife's soul and the soul of our unborn child helped her always feel well, secure, calm, and without abnormal worries. As we know, sometimes due to physical or spiritual challenges, pregnancy can result in abortion.

It's worth mentioning, briefly, that it is written in the *Zohar* that a woman screams and cries 70 times while giving birth; this is considered a form of prayer. Some recommend reciting Psalm 100 in order to give birth easily and without much pain.

Spiritual Dynamism

A particular person's spiritual system, as well as society's spiritual system, is in a permanent state of development and movement. The Creator constantly impacts us, day by day and minute by minute. For this simple but important reason, our task is to correct ourselves more and more at every moment.

As we mentioned, our ego will continue growing day after day, along with the collective ego and the global society's ego. We have no other option than to proactively correct and perfect our souls at all times.

The dynamism of the spiritual system can be compared to a person who decides to go up a down escalator. If we ascend at the same rate as the escalator (which is descending), we won't go up, but neither will we go down. If we climb faster than the escalator descends, we can make spiritual progress. But if on the other hand, our advance is slow or none, we will descend, and suffering will not be far behind.

Birthdays

As adults, we wonder why we celebrate people when they reach another birthday.

It's not a trivial question. It is reasonable because, at first glance, there's no reason to celebrate someone for the fact of having added another year of life and having one less to live. We're aware that the person has gotten older and their health tends to get worse over time. In this reality, it's clear that there's no good reason to celebrate when someone has increased their age.

More than 25 years ago I heard Rabbi Menachem Bernstein in Toronto, Canada explain why we celebrate people when they turn another year older.

Every year that passes, an individual's soul completes a spiritual cycle. From the day we're born and until we complete each year, our souls experience what we call an "ascent" (*aliá* in Hebrew), that is, the Kli becomes "broader". Due to this increase of Light, the Kli, by each birthday, can take in and hold more Light than it could the year before, because there's more "space" so more Light can enter. In this way, our soul rises a spiritual level and we receive greater influence, efficacy, and spiritual force in everything from that day forward.

When we receive an *aliá*, we find ourselves close to the Creator, and when we are closer to Him, He hears us in a louder voice, with more force and clarity.

This is why we customarily celebrate people on their birthdays. The Creator hears us better with every passing year, and therefore there is a higher probability that our clamoring will be answered every additional year. Many happy returns! Happy birthday!

Life and Death

We tend to perceive life in terms of births and deaths. We live to be able to finish the month on the money we have, uncertain what might happen to us if we don't or can't complete something. In short, the world and our lives are controlled by fear. Fear of the unknown, fear of death.

And what is death? Death is simply the necessary final step in the process of purifying the soul, or of rectifying the soul. Consequently, death is positive for a person's soul, because it's an opportunity to clean themselves of impurities, as well as being the moment when all the good things we did in life will accompany us and illuminate the path during the following stage, the next world.

The spiritual system is one, so all conflicts are the same at the root: friction or fights within a family are, on a different scale, like wars between nations. Each person is an independent entity, like a nation. Likewise, each nation is a spiritual entity and as such, has its own unique domain and its "luck" (the nation's soul) which rules it, just like any person.

The duality between life and death shows us that, death can come at any time.

It doesn't matter how long we live. The question is how much we have lived alive, and if we have made enough effort and fought to reach spirituality. Have we wanted it? Anyone who seeks spirituality knows that life doesn't end with death.

Chapter 5. Elements of the Spiritual Model

The spiritual system proposed here is composed of different parts that, together, show us how the Spiritual Light interacts with the Kli.

In Chapter 3 we briefly mentioned the concepts of desire and soul. We'll now address the classification and the details of these components of the spiritual model.

The concepts we will define below are:

1. Fields or spheres of desire—how we perceive the spiritual world we live in.
2. Levels or subdivisions of the soul.
3. Attributes or clothing of the Spiritual Light (sefirot in Hebrew) that act on the Kli's desires, correcting or changing them.

Spheres of Desire: The World We Perceive

The sensation of being surrounded by a large, diverse, and multifaceted world comes from the fact that our desires are still not fully corrected. After all, we live within them, as they were the only thing implanted within us by the Creator.

As we've explained, everything is within us, and what we see and feel "outside" our internal space also belongs to us.

Each of us has different types of desires, and we should understand what we can do with them. Some may also awaken within us that even we don't understand. The Spiritual Light that reaches us may be insufficient to focus all the desires in all their details, and therefore we should accept compromises to be able to modify them.

The question is, how do we perceive the spiritual world we live in?

There are five spheres, realms, or fields of desire (here with their Hebrew names in parenthesis), namely:

    A. Root (*shoresh*)

    B. Soul, breath (*neshamá*)

    C. Body (*guf*)

    D. Clothing (*levush*)

    E. External enclosure, residence, or palace (*heichal*)

These five spheres or fields can be subdivided into two groups.

Internal Desires

These are the desires we can feel, or "clear" desires within us. Desires perceived in our internal world. The internal desires are:

- o   Root
- o   Soul
- o   Body

The sphere called "root" is the germ or spark that initiates our desires. It is the part emitted by the general universal soul, the part from the soul of Adam, the first man with spiritual DNA, the purest and closest image of the Creator.

The "soul" sphere contains our conscious desires and the perception of our spiritual aspect.

The sphere known as "body" contains the desires and needs of our physical body and its functions in the world around us: inanimate objects, plants, and animals.

External Desires

These desires can't be felt directly, as if they weren't truly our desires. We perceive them as outside ourselves, as if they don't belong to us. But the desires perceived in the world around us also belong to us. The external desires are:

- o Clothing
- o External enclosure, residence, or palace

The sphere called "clothing" is the one that, although it is found outside the body, is attached to our being in relation to others. They are the desires related to our image or social and personal position, to what a person is and what a person wants to project (real or fictional) to those around them. For example, I want to demonstrate to myself and to those around me that I am an upright, trustworthy person, or a nuclear engineer, a boss who shows leadership, a professional who is self-assured, an honorable person, a professor or learned person, an eccentric magnate, a fool, an ignoramus, etcetera. Simply put, we dress ourselves in the desires we want to project from ourselves onto others. In this sphere we have the illusion of seeing before us friends, enemies, spectacles, and events to which we are witnesses.

The sphere called "residence"—external enclosure—is that which we clearly perceive outside ourselves. We feel a weak surrounding radiance and so we don't place too much spiritual weight on this phenomenon. We wrongly believe that, since we see them as far from us physically, they have nothing to do with us and are outside us, but it isn't so. Everything is within us. Some examples of these desires are: houses, buildings, mountains, the stars, the sun, the moon, their movement—zodiac—and the influence they have on us and the nature surrounding us. Everything has to do with us.

This division of our desires into five fields exists only in our perception; all are our desires and we must manage them to help correct them within ourselves. The day we reform all our desires so they join together inside us in a single altruistic, anti-egoistic action, we will find that the universe is within us.

We don't realize that all our desires, even those that our outside us, belong to us, though we have the illusion that they are external and separate.

I am all my desires.

Who do we marry? Our desires.

Who makes us laugh? Our desires.

Who do we argue with? Our desires.

Soul Levels or Intensities

As we discussed in chapter 3, the Spiritual Light shines inside the Kli. We call this light the soul, and according to the quality of its spiritual intensity, we subdivide souls into five parts, or levels, which we explain below.

These five parts are five grades of Spiritual Light. Each level is identified with a spiritual aspect of the individual. If we combine the particular details of the Light in each of the levels, despite the fact that they can sometimes contradict each other, they will give us the power and force of unity—unitary, unique, and unified—which will reveal the Spiritual Light to us fully.

The five spiritual levels of the soul are, in order of intensity from least to most intense, the following (with Hebrew names in parenthesis):

1) Resident soul, action; Light of the "inanimate" part of the human body (*néfesh*).
2) Spirit, speech; Light of the "vegetable" part of the human body (*rúach*).
3) Divine soul, though; Light of the "animate" part of the human body (*neshamá*).

4) Living essence, mind; Light of the "speaking" part of the human body (*chayá*).

5) Unique essence, volition, ray of the infinite (*yechidá*).

It can be seen that the three first–*néfesh*, *rúach* and neshamá—are the imminent levels of the soul, that is to say that they are levels inherent to the individual, not the result of external actions. In psychological terms, we could make a parallel with the subconscious, the consciousness, and the superego.

Of the other levels, *chayá* and *yechidá*, we can say they are the levels that surround higher consciousness.

Each of these levels is dynamic and presents movement and comings and goings. There are transitions and vibrations in each of them. All are interconnected with each other, and each increases intensity or quality of Light, growing until the final correction of our soul is achieved. It's worth mentioning that in order to reach this point we will have experienced and overcome all types of changes and transformations that kept us from union with the only and total Light before. Independent of these changes and transformations, we should still be able to join, filling our Kli with the one unified Light.

Explanations:

Néfesh

This is the lowest grade, the Light of least intensity, the most tenuous, the Light of the resident soul. There is a revelation of Light even at this level, although this intensity of light does not result in any transformation. Each of us has a minimal, "immobile" spiritual condition of Light, and each of us seeks to connect with others. This is the Light of basic unification, the "inanimate."

Rúach

Going up a level, each part of the Light begins to transform. By remaining united, the changes and comings and goings of this level of spiritual force don't reveal the next level of intensity of Light.

At the *rúach* level we can begin to see the transformation of our individual properties. It is the same Light of unification, but at a higher level; we pass from the "inanimate" level to the second level of spiritual power, the "vegetable."

Neshamá

Rising another level and maintaining the same Light of unification—unitary, unique, and unified—the Light increases its intensity and quality. Depending on the spiritual grade of the person, the Light moves to the third level, the "animated" – *neshamá*—where the spiritual force begins to move freely in relationships with others. Our force flows back and forth among individuals.

Chayá

The next level of the soul is called *chayá*. It is the fourth level, the "speaking" level, where we begin to communicate spiritually as if we all belonged to one body.

Yechidá

Finally, the fifth and last level of spiritual force is the divine level. "Infinite Light," intense and refined—*yechidá*—which consolidates perfect spiritual unity. When we reach this level we are able to influence everyone in everything, as if we were the Creator's essence itself, and this marks the end of our soul's correction. This final level of the soul is the part of our spiritual DNA which makes us like the essence of the Creator and which we all carry etched inside us.

Sefirot: Attributes of the Spiritual Light Reflected in the Kli

As we mentioned in Chapter 3, the Kli is divided into parts with different levels of "refinement" or different "thicknesses." The Kli receives every one of the five levels of Spiritual Light according to its thickness or refinement. The Spiritual light shines within the Kli with ten different intensities or attributes called *sefirot*.

The *sefirot* "clothes" the Kli in these different attributes or "clothes" of spiritual energy to influence a person's desires. These can be corrected, depending on the intensity or force that the Spiritual Light influences on them.

Sefirá (singular of *sefirot*) has various meanings:

a) Count or enumeration;

b) It comes from the word "sapphire;" the term connotes illumination, brilliance, or shine;

c) Story, expression, communication;

d) Limit;

e) Revelation.

There are ten (10) *sefirot*. The Spiritual Light –which is very strong—can be compared to the sunlight passing through "filters" that have different attributes and characteristics which create changes in desire. The Light must always pass through these filters; there's no way to receive it directly. The ten *sefirot* are like a ray of light passing through a prism. A ray of light enters in one side of the prism and on the other side it exits divided into a fan of seven colors. A person perceives them as if they were lights of various shades, when in reality it is one light. The multicolored rainbow is a distortion created by the prism.

Each *sefirá* shows its splendor or "shine" when a person yearns to follow the actions of the Light on the Kli. This means that the sefirot dress themselves in the desires of the person, helping him in the process of changing, in the transformation of the spiritual body to its state of influence. The Light, upon affecting desire, will bring new ideas, knowledge, and sensations, and it will also reveal a world that is completely new to us. The level of influence the Light has to correct desire in a person is that person's level of spirituality.

These ten creative forces are what connects the infinite Light of the Creator to us and to our world. All this through the Kli. The Kabbalistic tradition generally talks about ten *sefirot*. But occasionally a total of eleven *sefirot* are counted, as two of them represent different dimensions of a single force.

Some people refer to the sefirot as the form or attributes through which the Creator manifests Himself and communicates with his Creation. But it must be made clear that the sefirot aren't the Creator, they are the medium through which the qualities and attributes specific to Him may be manifested.

The following are the *sefirot* (with their Hebrew names listed in parentheses) listed in order of greatest to least proximity to the Creator, from least thickness (the most pure, finest) to most thickness (most impure), from top to bottom:

Note: on this list we include *sefirá* #11 (**)

- "Crown:" the spark or point where everything begins (*keter*) is the finest or thinnest of the *sefirot* (*)
- "Wisdom:" conception, seed, the aha! moment (*chochmá*).
- "Understanding:" comprehension, articulation, construction, elaboration (*biná*).
- "Knowledge:" application, internalization (*daat*) (** *sefirá* #11).
- "Kindness:" love, attraction, unconditional acceptance (*chésed*).

- "Judgement:" power, force, severity, discipline, obligations, limits (*gevurá*).
- "Beauty:" harmony, glory, empathy, compassion (*tiferet*).
- "Victory:" ambition, strength (*netzach*).
- "Splendor:" devotion, humility (*hod*).
- "Foundation:" cement, base, connection (*yesod* ***).
- "Kingdom:" sovereignty, divine presence, faith (*malchut*), the thickest and coarsest of the *sefirot*.

As we mentioned earlier, two of them ("crown" and "knowledge") represent different dimensions of one force, and therefore *sefirá* #11, "knowledge" is sometimes omitted.

(*) Regarding *keter* or "crown", we can add that it is the volitional power that comes from our divine essence. When we are connected, we can move mountains. Sometimes we cannot fulfill our will, but no one can take it from us.

(***) Balancing the forces of *netzach* and *hod* establishes a solid *yesod*, or cement, "foundation" in life.

The *yesod* channels the eight energies that precede it (from "wisdom" to "splendor"), in order to afterwards share them with *malchut* as the final stage of spirituality.

111

It's important to note that the following group of six *sefirot—chésed, gevurá, tiferet, netzach, hod* and *yesod*—are also called *zeir-anpin* (a Hebrew word that means "Little face"). These sefirot can be grouped together because at times certain activities of the Spiritual Light are common to the whole group. This is why they are referred to as one.

Internally, each *sefirá* is also subdivided into ten different *sefirot*. Example: the *sefirá malchut* has within it the ten *sefirot* (*keter, chochmá, biná, zeir-anpin, malchut*), and they are called *malchut* of *keter, malchut* of *jojmá, malchut* of *biná*, etc. The internal study of each sefirá isn't part of this introductory book.

The *sefirot* can further be classified, according to their characteristics, in three columns (see figure 2):

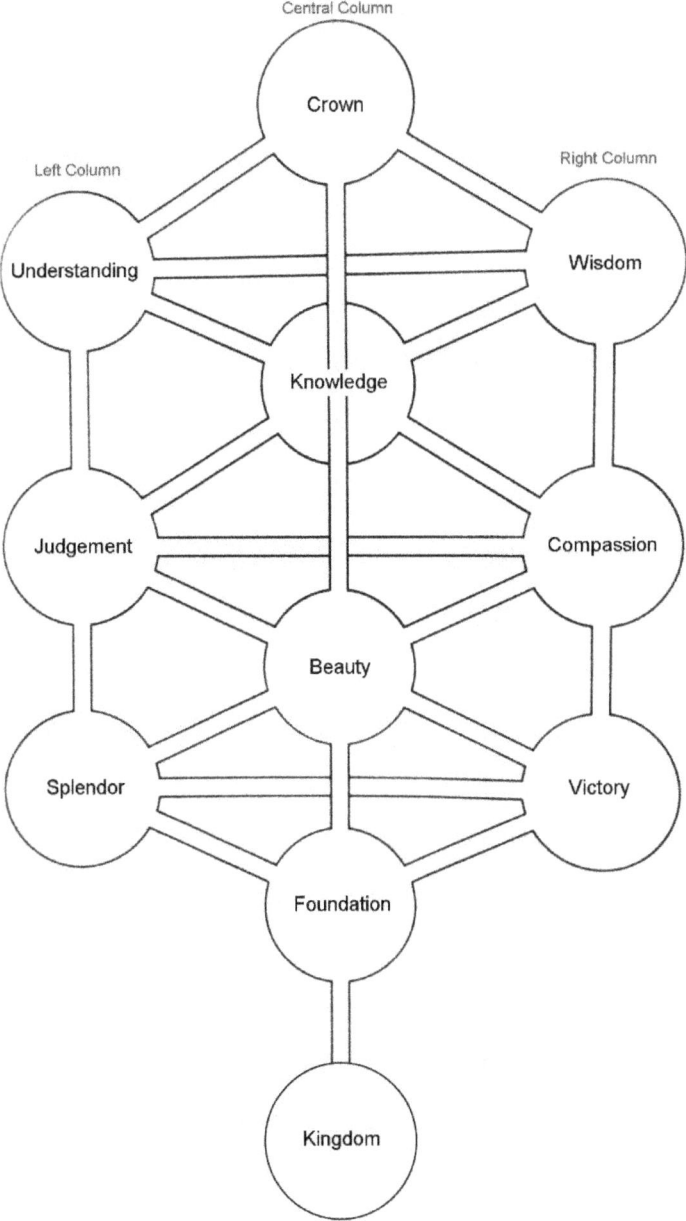

Central Column

Crown

Left Column   Right Column

Understanding   Wisdom

Knowledge

Judgement   Compassion

Beauty

Splendor   Victory

Foundation

Kingdom

The Sefirot

- The right column or line= wisdom, compassion, love and unconditional acceptance, victory.

-The left column or line= understanding, judgement, severity, discipline, creativity, obligations, limits, splendor.

- The center column or line= crown, knowledge, beauty, foundation, and kingdom.

Spiritual Balance among the Columns

The goal of spiritual activity is a perfect balance among the sefirot corresponding to the left and right columns. The balance is expressed in the *sefirot* corresponding to the central column.

The central column synthesizes the forces of the right and left, generating harmony, unity, and peace, and putting the ten *sefirot* in their correct states. Correcting the central column, that is, balancing the left and right, is the end and goal of our improvement.

When we say balance, that doesn't mean a strict 50-50 division. The characteristics in the right column should have primacy over those of the left column. The division could be anything, 85-15, 60-40, 56-44, etc. it doesn't need to be a particular ratio. The important thing is to come to a point of equilibrium between the spiritual force on the right and the spiritual force on the left. We can see these columns reflected in everything around us, in nature and in society.

Our spiritual DNA has many "genes," and each of them is a desire or inclination shaped by the ten attributes or *sefirot*. Each "gene" has its own sefirot topography, which is to say each *sefirá* (illumination) has a specific value, height, intensity or "quantity" according to the desire and the person. The "quantity" of spiritual energy in each *sefirá* varies with each object, individual, and group. Our job, as individuals, a community, and a society, is to balance our two columns (left and right), so that there can be a connection between the characteristics of the Creator in our spiritual DNA toward our neighbors. Likewise, we will also need to make adjustments within ourselves towards others and our partner or group, that is, a balance of the parts involved in the characteristics of the Creator.

For example: we ask, how should a father raise a child? If the father only shows love and affection indiscriminately, that is, he only uses the illumination of kindness (*chésed*), without restrictions or limits, without severity or discipline, without the necessary amount of the illumination of judgement, obligations, and limits (*gevurá*), then the child's upbringing will be terrible and he will be spoiled.

We can also refer to politics, to the movements of the Left and Right. Both are necessary for a country's normal development. But if they don't occasionally reach compromises that balance these two sometimes apparently incompatible positions then political instability will result. This is reflected when the political system in power at the time isn't conducive to the real spiritual balance that should exist at the socioeconomic juncture in which it is situated. Democratic governments that work only on absolute majority (50% +1) are not usually efficient, urgent changes are delayed, there are steps backwards, the country doesn't move forward or develop the way it should. This type of democracy doesn't take into account the balance of spiritual forces. A democracy must be created with a spiritual balance between the forces of the Right and the Left so that things flow and the country progresses in social and economic well-being to the benefit of all its inhabitants.

We'll leave this controversial, passionate, and critical issue on hold for another forum.

The Relationship between the Levels of the Soul (Light) and the *Sefirot* (Kli)

The Light and its five levels correspond to the illuminations of the Kli in the following way:

- *Keter* (the finest *sefirá*) ←→ *Yechidá* (the most intense, refined Light)

  When the Light is very intense and refined, it can only dress the finest part of the Kli. When the Kli is thick and coarse, it can't take advantage of a refined Light.

- *Chochmá* ←→ *Chayá*

- *Biná* ←→ *Neshamá*

- *Zeir-anpin* (*chésed, gevurá, tiferet, netzach, hod* and *yesod*) ←→ *Rúach*

- *Malchut* (the coarsest *sefirá*) ←→ *Néfesh* (The weakest, least intense Light)

  The most refined Light cannot dress the coarsest part of the Kli, it is wasted. Only a tenuous, weak Light can do so.

117

Chapter 6. Us

In this chapter we will describe the elements and characteristics needed for us, both individually and collectively, to be able to actively embark on our spiritual preparation, awareness, and readiness.

The Individual

As individuals, we should propose to live a life of peace, tranquility, and love, in total coordination of body and soul, in order to make our goals, both material and spiritual, a reality. We have already said that the individual is the atom of any spiritual relationship. Spiritual reality is only revealed in a binary spiritual relationship between, at a minimum, two individuals under reciprocal conditions. The "spiritual molecule" is composed of two atoms, two individuals: the one who gives and the one who receives.

The intangible or immaterial aspects of the individual (psychological, mental, intellectual, emotional, and social) allow them to establish and in a large part determine the composition of their spiritual system.

The individual's concern is to stay alert and aware of everything that happens in the present, in their now, with the force or will and discipline to overcome past events or thoughts about the future that influence their emotions, compromising decisions they make in the present.

The clear goal while we are living is to complete the correction (in Hebrew, *tikún*) of our spiritual DNA or in other words the balance between left and right before we reach the end of the physical road: death.

Personal Benefit

And so we ask ourselves, how does it help a person to emphasize spirituality and give priority to their spiritual aspect? What do they get in return? What do they gain by advancing spiritually?

By reaching a higher spiritual level than the one they are currently in, a person obtains the clear perception of a privileged reality, in addition to getting closer to the goal, eternal, perfect life.

So what is this clear spiritual experience? How is it manifested in a person? What are the "symptoms"?

When we experience a step up in our spirituality, we vibrate with more intensity, and we are more attentive and sensitive to details of daily life. They are experiences that connect us to a present free from past and future influences. This intense present, which we were unaware of before, is now revealed to us more clearly, as much physically as intellectually and emotionally. The quality and amount of details in our daily life will generate a more influential spiritual result.

Groups or Associations

The relationship between two people—a binary relationship—is the minimum expression of a group or team. When two or more people come together, each of them can develop their own spiritual relationship with their neighbor, which will benefit the spiritual project. We should commit all our talents to the benefit of the members of the group.

Building a good group isn't easy. At least one member needs to be solidly familiar with how to manage a present without emotional influences in order to be able to conduct group discussions in a way that maintains the necessary conditions, such as mutual trust and a clear desire for spirituality inside oneself. If not, the mind, which is naturally egotistical, will sabotage any spiritual advance.

Community work is invaluable for spiritual growth, but not sufficient. One cannot depend only on group work, nor on a teacher or spiritual guide, except at the beginning or during stages of transition while one is learning and practicing, as we'll see later on.

It's advisable to avoid as much as possible conflict between people due to mind-to-mind or ego-to-ego interactions, because they will affect the group's spiritual progress. There are times when it is necessary to solve personal conflict individually and privately for the sake of the common good and the spiritual work. It's helpful to practice person-to-person communication, or interpersonal communion, thereby creating a space for the relationship in our present. Groups are important because an extended desire, composed of all the desires of the individuals together, will appear inside each of the group's members via the group.

"I want you desires, do you need mine? I'm ready, take them. But first let's connect ourselves where we all want to connect our hearts."

The spiritual desires of this team of people are united to create a single, much larger desire, complete, and of a higher spiritual quality, which groups together all the members' desires and represents each and every one of the members. That is, a group Kli is formed, obviously much larger than each individual's Kli, and also larger than the sum of the Kelim. And of course, with a larger Kli, our power of influence grows proportionally.

Mutual Guarantee (*Arvut*)

Mutual guarantee (*arvut*, in Hebrew) is the relationship or interconnection and independence that a team has, as part of a unique spiritual project in which we are all "organs" in one body.

My obligation, as someone's spiritual partner or as a member of a community or team doing spiritual work is to make, maintain, consider, and guarantee a continual relationship with each and every member of the group.

What is my obligation toward my group or partner?

It is written in the *Talmud* (Sanhedrin 27:72) that "All Israel is responsible for one another." Likewise, we have the precepts to "love thy neighbor as thyself" and "do not do unto others what you would not have done unto you."

This means that each and every one of us in Israel (those who are oriented "directly at the Creator") take on the responsibility of helping, caring for, affirming, working for and with every one of the members of our partnerships, groups, communities, or nations, in order to resolve and satisfy their true needs and desires.

A person cannot reach the desired goal on the spiritual path without the connection and help of those around them.

Love in Relationships

Love may come and stay for a while, but eventually it usually disappears. Why? The reason is that real love is part of a natural internal state within a person. This passing love was created by an external stimulus and not from within the individual.

Real love is a-temporal and not based on appearances or emotions, it doesn't judge in any way, it has no thoughts of the past or the future to influence it. Loving with the ego is called interested influence, and involves receiving something in return, that is, it is motivated by the need to receive. Loving without the ego, we yield our identities. This is spiritual love, and real love. Any other way would not be real love. This means that we give the Light we have received completely to the loved person, without keeping anything back; it means that we become transparent, without manifesting our ego in any way.

When we truly love someone, we are fulfilled by simply the feeling of love, or influence, we feel toward our partner or the beloved person. Even if these feelings aren't reciprocated, and the person who is loved does not love in return, having influence and real love for someone fills us with full satisfaction and our Kli will be fulfilled (*milúi*, in Hebrew) the benefit of spiritual growth from loving is for the one who loves, not necessarily for the one who is loved. Obviously, real, reciprocated love is the ideal state.

If we make ourselves a portal through which our internal divinity shines, there is no need to search for love, it will come without fail.

The unification between the body and spirit is the perfect, ultimate sexual practice. The culminating phase of our sexual evolution requires the connection of the body, and physical sense to our emotional and spiritual being.

Compassion is a sentiment close to love. Compassion is the awareness of a profound connection between a person and their neighbor and between a person and all the beings in the universe. True compassion is being conscious of the common, shared link of mortality as well as immortality. Compassion isn't only measured by doing things for others, but also by being fully present, conscious, with integrity, for that person. We must rise to the level at which two souls become coordinated and then in a state of arvut—or mutual guarantee—we can achieve spiritual balance.

Choosing or Forming a Team

The social environment in which we develop and live is fundamental to our spiritual growth. We are products and consequences of the society we live in.

Many people are captives of society, with few options for escape. It is therefore vitally important to live and keep oneself in a community with high moral standards, because we will be a product of that entity.

It is written in the sacred scriptures: "Get yourself a teacher and acquire a friend."

In contrast to "getting" the teacher, we say "acquire" a friend, referring to the fact that between friends there must be a clear, manifest interest in gaining something—whether it be via tangible or intangible gifts—from one another. When there is a constant shared interest between friends, the friendship can become honest and lasting. If there is no mutually-beneficial transaction, the relationship is illusory and ruled by appearances or social and/or cultural convenience.

It is our duty to build an environment which will guide us to use society as reinforcement to accelerate our spiritual progress.

If, for example, we need money for a project for social good, we can surround ourselves with people who support it and work for it, and with whom we can talk about it; this will inspire us to work hard. Or, for example, if we want to lose weight, the easiest way to do so is to surround ourselves with people who think about, talk about, and have decided to lose weight. Actually, we can do even more to create an environment, such as reinforcing that environment with books, movies, talks, seminars, classes, and articles.

All this occurs within in the environment in which we find ourselves. For example, Alcoholics Anonymous and drug rehab centers use the power of community to help people when they can't help themselves. If we use our environment correctly, we will achieve things we never even dreamed were possible.

The desire to understand the spiritual system is no exception. If we aspire to spirituality and to increasing our access to and desire for it, we only need appropriate friends, texts, and teachers around us. The divine part of our spiritual DNA will do the rest.

Examples of Groups with Spiritual Foundations

The common denominator of societies, countries, civilizations, peoples, or tribes is the fight for social, intellectual, cultural, emotional, and economic power over others, which is expressed in the human behaviors of conquest, power, and other types of imperialist desire.

But when the common denominator is a connection through a spiritual project or work, there is no competition for influence: each person has their own part which brings them satisfaction (*sipúk*, in Hebrew), pleasure, and benefit, both to the community and the group.

We can list a few examples of groups with spiritual projects:

- Natural spiritual unions, like the relationships between parents and children, husband and wife, family, friends, etc.

- Organizations with spiritual content, an identity, and a purpose, established for the benefit of the citizens, such as the government, its organizations and public companies, non-profit organizations, colleges and universities, social support funds from public and private businesses, etc.

- Virtual groups based on spiritual projects on social media, chats, email, and other electronic, and cybernetic applications.

Note that we should be constantly reaffirming that the spiritual project will benefit the community, because there is a real possibility that the work may turn into a relationship for economic interest or become motivated by trafficking in personal influence, negating the spiritual effect and diverting us once again towards competing egotistically for ourselves.

Chapter 7. Spiritual Progress

In this chapter, we will lay out clearly and concisely the steps to follow to achieve the spiritual success which will lead us to a life of peace, tranquility and love, to realize all our desires, whether tangible or intangible, material or spiritual, intellectual or physical.

The Path to Spiritual Success

Spiritual success implies control and presence in our lives at a personal level, influence at the social level (family, community, and world) and living in an integrated way, satisfied with what we have, in harmony with the ecosystem and the pleasure of sharing what we achieve.

The road to spiritual success should be a gratifying route which brings happiness with every step we take and each level we reach, until we reach the goal we desire.

Goals to Achieve

Spiritual progress occurs through reaching these two goals:

A. Connection with a person or group of people.
A state of influence is obtained by imitating the actions of the Creator; it can be achieved only in

relationship with another person or a group. This connection facilitates the state of influence and completes the capacity to achieve and satisfy a latent desire or need inside oneself.

B. Acquisition of the essence of the Creator Himself Proclaiming the necessity of achieving the purpose of the Creator is a formal petition to receive the Spiritual Light. Each person determines what they will receive according to their own spiritual DNA, and to their capacity, that is, according to their similarity to the essence of the Creator or their equivalence of form with the Creator.

Individual Progress

An individual's private activities, such as praying, meditating, studying, and reading about spirituality or related topics are fundamental to achieve success in our spiritual progress.

For individual progress, studying texts related to the spiritual system (Kabbalah) is vital. The individual, like a group, will need to study texts that immerse them in the topic.

In the same vein, it is important to correct and improve interpersonal relations as much as possible, in a parallel, independent manner to the spiritual relationship with their partner or team. If necessary, their psychological, motivational, organizational attributes, as well as their social behavior must also be corrected and improved in order to facilitate as much as possible achieving our goal: spiritual projects which will result in general well-being.

The capacity for individual change in all people is important, positive, and directly influences the spiritual connection between them and their group-mates, the beneficiaries of the spiritual project, and society in general. The idea is that each individual—in their interpersonal relationships, in spiritual projects—can exude ease of connection and communication with people. Any personal improvement in any area is welcome as a way to improve spiritual connection. We can advance in this area through self-study, reading, internet courses, mobile applications, encounters, and seminars. All this in order to further spiritual works.

It's important to note that the group in and of itself doesn't determine the quantity or quality of Spiritual Light, nor the type or influence that will be received. The quality, quantity, and type of influence of the Spiritual Light which comes to each person will be in accord with their spiritual level. People can't choose what we want to receive nor what we want influence over. We can only intervene in the path or manner of progress in our spiritual journeys, in other words, we choose which road to take to get closer and closer to understanding and managing our spiritual system.

We insist (in the form of spoken or silent prayer) on receiving more Light. But receiving Spiritual Light doesn't depend of the group or partner, but on the type and quality of connection which we as individuals maintain with our spiritual projects, their beneficiaries, and with each of the people in the team; it's not a question of the number of people with whom we are connected, but of the quality of each connection.

Methods of Spiritual Progress

All the people on the planet are constantly progressing spiritually, although at times it may be very slow and not very noticeable. As we already mentioned in the section on spiritual dynamism, the natural progress of Civilization toward spirituality occurs at a very slow pace, while the growth of the universal ego occurs more quickly.

In general, the vast majority of people, who aren't yet conscious of the spiritual system, evolve spiritually in an inertial way, very slowly, at the pace of society, without any special effort and without the purpose of seeking spirituality. When we advance this way, we are faced with situations that cause suffering, punishments, natural disasters and so many other unexpected misfortunes. These are reactions to spiritual inactivity, leaving aside the goal of imitating the Creator.

It's like any living body: we if we don't feed out spirituality, we will experience afflictions that we could have avoided. Therefore we have no other remedy but to advance our spirituality at a faster pace than that of our accelerated, inflated ego.

We can organize spiritual progress into two styles or different behaviors:

a) The reactive style, driven by suffering, very slowly, or

b) The proactive style that is guided by the spiritual work we are developing, in an accelerated manner.

We can decide whether we advance quickly (for better) or slowly (for worse).

There will always be progress. The question is how to adapt it to our lives: if we try to learn and to hold firm to the purpose of moving ourselves in the direction of the Creator, which will be much faster, or on the other hand, if we are going to stagnate or regress and advance only when forced by whip lashes and disasters. This is the normal pace in our time and the common pace of our Civilization over the last centuries.

Chapter 8. Spiritual Model

The spiritual model contains entities, and these are defined here:

Entities of the Proposed Spiritual Model

The basic, indispensable entities for the path to spiritual success are the following:

1. The **individual**: every one of us, the atom of the spiritual relationship

2. The **group** or team, which may be:
    - A binary relationship: one-to-one (between a couple, two friends, parent and child, teacher and student, two colleagues, etc.);
    - A one-to-many relationship (between teacher and students, boss and employees, captain and soldiers, one person and their congregation, etc.)
    - A many-to-many relationship (among the members of a troupe, among the players on a soccer team, among various groups, among family members, etc.).

3. The **teacher**, leader, mentor, or spiritual guide.

4. **Study and reading** documents written about the spiritual system.

5. The **spiritual project**: projects or works which influence one or more people through assistance or other acts of kindness. The implementation of a spiritual project, the work in progress, feeds back into the spiritual systems of the participants.

Among each of these entities there are relationships with conditions that must be fulfilled, tasks to carry out, and goals to reach for a spiritual project to be implemented.

The spiritual model proposed here is composed of two circles or areas, namely:

I.   Circle of preparation and start-up.

II.   Circle of spiritual action, progress, and evaluation.

We will explain the parts, elements, events and activities, conditions of operation, and goals of each circle.

Circle I: Preparation and Start-up

Circle I is the circle of preparation and start-up, in which a person begins the process of study and immersion in the spiritual system. This circle includes the following entities:

1. Teacher (**T**)

2. Study (**S**)

3. Individual (**I**)

4. Group (**G**)

These four entities should be established at the beginning of any spiritual project.

As we mentioned before, we come to this circle at the beginning of our spiritual road. But there are also moments when a person in Circle II needs to do activities from Circle I, such as finding another teacher because the existing teacher is no longer available, or finding a new team or partner.

Guide to Relationships among the Entities in Circle I

The entities in Circle I are related to one another through events and activities in the following way (figure 3):

- One (1) teacher can teach and guide many (N) individuals (1→N relationship)
- One (1) teacher can teach using many texts (1→N relationship)
- One (1) teacher can teach or guide various teams (1→N relationship)

- One (1) individual can belong to various groups and in one group there may be two or more individuals (M←→N relationship)
- One (1) individual can study various texts or sources and 1 text is studied by many individuals (M←→N relationship)

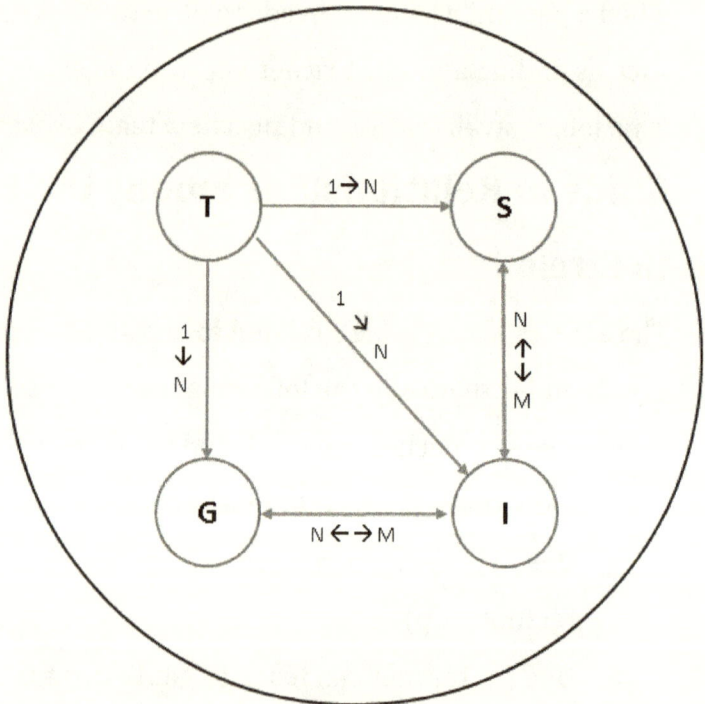

Circle I

Figure 3

For a clearer understanding we include figure 4, which is a summary of the four Circle I entities, and synthesizes figure 3.

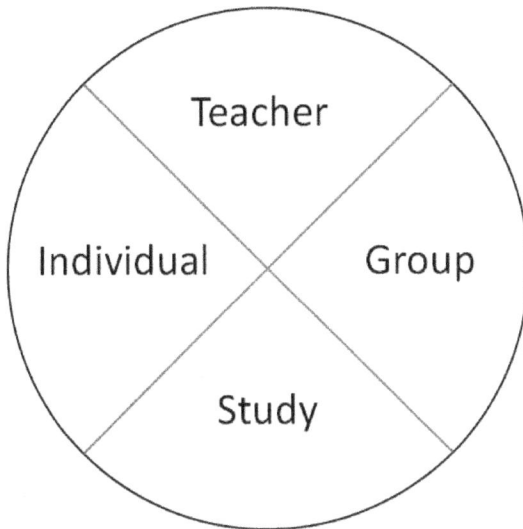

Entities Circle I
Figure 4

Teacher, Leader, or Spiritual Guide

Find a teacher, leader, or spiritual guide, is one of the basic entities of Circle I.

The teacher should teach methods for working with the Spiritual Light, written in sacred texts on the topic.

As we mentioned before, it is written in the sacred scriptures, "Get yourself a Teacher and acquire a friend."

The teacher should be someone we can revere, admire, and see as someone with a greater and better understanding of the spiritual, who can guide and teach us, like a parent guides and teaches a child.

Occasionally, the teacher may also be, in turn, a friend who must be "acquired." The main thing is that they have more knowledge and experience with the spiritual system and how it works.

The teacher should stay with the students whenever they need him. As soon as this need disappears, the next teacher will come to those students who are ready.

The teacher's goal is to teach his disciples the basic rules and the behavior of the spiritual forces that the person begins to learn and to think about, both independently and with a group, using spiritual terms. In this way, they will learn to distinguish and apply what is already written in books and primary sources.

The student may follow the teacher for life, if desired.

Studying Texts Related to the Spiritual Model

Studying and reading books, texts, and documents related to the topic is another entity in Circle I. This activity is parallel to acquiring a teacher, because they go together and one complements the other: the teacher teaches us according to books and sacred texts.

As we begin to learn about spirituality, it's logical and natural that we should study sacred books in which the spiritual system is explained for different levels of understanding. There are some people who start studying basic sacred books, according to their level of comprehension, explication, and interpretation, such as, for example:

1) The *Tanach* –which includes: the Pentateuch (*Torá* in Hebrew), the prophets and the scribes— texts on a simple level.

2) The *Mishná*, gematria, more sophisticated texts, texts with advice and suggestions.

3) The *Talmud*, high-level texts that are discussed, debated, argued about, searched, refuted and questioned.

4) The *Zohar*, abstract texts that give spiritual explications of physical activities, texts with revelations, esoteric texts

with secrets and mysteries that explain writings at other

levels, and which explain the spiritual system in detail.

The book that brought all the secrets of the spiritual system

is the famous book of *Zohar* (Splendor) written by Rabbi

Shimón Bar Yohai (nicknamed "Rashbi"), in the 2nd century

C.E. It's worth mentioning that one of the first books about

spirituality and the basis of the book of *Zohar* is *Sefer*

Yetzirah, composed by the patriarch Abraham more than

3,000 years ago.

The *Zohar* is not for solitary study. Its teachings should be

passed from the teacher (Kabbalist) to the student. This is

why the study of the contents of the *Zohar* is called Kabbalah,

a Hebrew word that means reception. In other words, the

content is transmitted from the teacher –who has already

received the content—to the student. In Kabbalistic terms, a

spiritual teacher with many years of experience studying the

Zohar is called *mecubal* ("received" or "accepted"), meaning

they have already received the basic knowledge of the

spiritual system.

Reading the *Zohar* as if it was a regular, every day book

would make it incomprehensible. To assimilate it, one must

understand a basic introduction provided by the teacher,

during which the heart and soul of the person can begin to

absorb everything that the science of Kabbalah brings us, its demands, opinions, and perspectives about life and the world.

Since the *Zohar* was written, many Kabbalists have published several books of commentary regarding the spiritual system. We can mention some renowned Kabbalists, such as Rabbi Yehuda Ashlag (Baal Ha-Sulam), Nahmanides (Ramban), Moses Cordovero, Rabbi Isaac Luria or "Ha'ari" ("the lion") or just "Arizal," Haim Vital, Moses de Leon, the Maharal of Prague, Rabbi Moshe Haim Luzzatto, Rabbi Nachman of Breslov, Rabbi Shneur Zalman of Liadi, and other saints, pious and geniuses of the spiritual system.

Preparing the Individual

Another entity in Circle I is the way an individual prepares their present way of life. A person who already enjoys and understands their "point in the heart," the person who is conscious of their spiritual DNA and their divine "gene," consequently lives their life under specific conditions that orient them toward their spiritual goals.

It's up to individuals, outside of studying and finding a teacher, to help themselves to constantly ascend to higher spiritual levels through prayer in congregation, acts of kindness, helping neighbors, and volunteering for the benefit of society. It's worth noting that the individual, without needing a group or partner, can help people in need with acts of generosity, such as monetary donations toward spiritual causes or contributions of time dedicated to volunteer work in social collaboration projects.

As individuals, we should make an effort to understand and capitalize on all the facts and events presented to us in our daily lives.

The individual will little by little acquire the ability to understand the "topography" of their own spiritual system. Thanks to a basic understanding of the spiritual model, they will begin to live each moment of the day in good physical shape, with a defined purpose, with enthusiasm, influence, and persuasion, free of depression or other emotional problems, happy with what they have and gain, with clarity of thought, excellent productivity and energy in their daily work, a positive attitude, in companionship with their neighbors, with self-confidence, inspiring trust and admiration in others.

Joining a Team

Joining and forming relationships with a group or partner in order to work on large-scale spiritual projects is the other entity in Circle I.

The bigger the group is, the harder it is to create a state of mutual guarantee, arvut, among the members, but the greater the benefit. In Judaism, a minimum of ten men is required for group prayer. This fact is related to, among other things, the ten *sefirot*.

With the exception of a couple, in which there is already a shared relationship developed between two people—for example, a long-term couple, married or cohabitating—we recommend that teams be of one gender only, separated into men and women, to thereby try to avoid as much as possible any inconveniences due to romantic issues or issues of gender, which can interfere with the spiritual project. This recommendation, which shows modesty and humility, is a healthy, simple, unpretentious measure, which can help us get the best spiritual results as quickly as possible. To be clear, this depends on the age of the people in a group, for example elderly adults could form groups that include both genders. In our society there are many non-profit groups managed perfectly by one or two people, partners in a spiritual cause.

The ultimate spiritual goal for the team is to be interconnected as if we were a single body and a single shared soul, much bigger than that of each of the members, which includes everyone and in which we are all conscious of said integration and union. When this state of union is achieved, the infinite Spiritual Light will flow among all the members of the team without any limitations or exceptions. In order for the individual to understand what happens to them, to see clearly and transcend in a positive way the reality of the world around them, they should take advantage of the group as a platform from which all the desires of the group shine through. The group should give us the capacity to elevate and spotlight a latent need or desire within each and every one of us.

This is why the influence of the group or society on a person is the most important for our development, both spiritual and social.

As we've said in earlier chapters, we are prisoners of the society we live in. If a person is in a "harmful" or "damaging" enterprise, or one whose influence doesn't benefit them, the results will be of the same quality. If we have the luck and ability to choose, join, or surround ourselves with a collection of individuals who are conscious of their "points in the heart" and with spiritual interests like ours, the results for our spiritual advancement will be positive.

In this age when the internet is an integral part of our lives, in which thousands of apps like Facebook group together people and communities, the question is, can one belong to a virtual spiritual group? The basis of a team is direct integration among its members, which preferably requires the physical presence of a person. Once an association is established and working, virtual interaction does allow many aspects of the spiritual project to move forward.

The individual should stay in Circle I until advances in their spiritual reality begin to show, such as an increase in the level of basic influence in their spiritual relationships.

Circle II: Spiritual Action, Progress, and Evaluation

Circle II, spiritual action, progress, and evaluation, concerns the person who is beginning to reflect the Creator's essence in their spiritual relationships with their partner, family, and community. The individual already shows some revelation of the spiritual system within them.

This circle includes the following entities:

1. Circle I (**C1**)
2. Spiritual works/projects (**SP**)
3. Beneficiaries of the spiritual work, neighbor (**B**)

We reach this circle once Circle I is already established, which now starts to become part of Circle II. As we mentioned before, there are times when a person in Circle II needs to do activities from Circle I.

Circle II includes the final steps in the system, which should be repeated continually until the highest level of spirituality is reached, which is when the person's soul is completely corrected and the Law of Equivalence of Form is absolute: the end of our correction.

Guide to Relationships among the Entities in Circle II

The entities in Circle II are interrelated through events and activities in the following manner (figure 5):

- One (1) Circle 1 can participate in many (N) spiritual projects (1➔N relationship)
- One (1) Circle I can benefit many people (1➔N relationship)

- One (1) spiritual work or project can benefit various people and one (1) person can receive benefits from various spiritual projects (N←→M relationship)

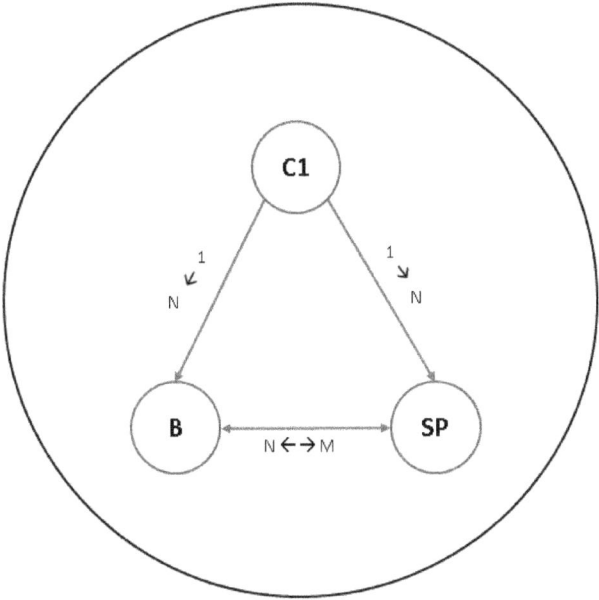

Circle II

Figure 5

The entities in Circle II are those that give us the information to carry out spiritual projects and work.

Within Circle II there are activities we should complete to measure our spiritual progress, evaluate our influence on our neighbors, reflect to maintain our current spiritual level, and correct details necessary for our continued growth.

Below we present a diagram that shows Circle II activities.

Circle II Activities Flowchart

The following is a flowchart showing the activities of each entity in Circle II and how our spiritual model works:

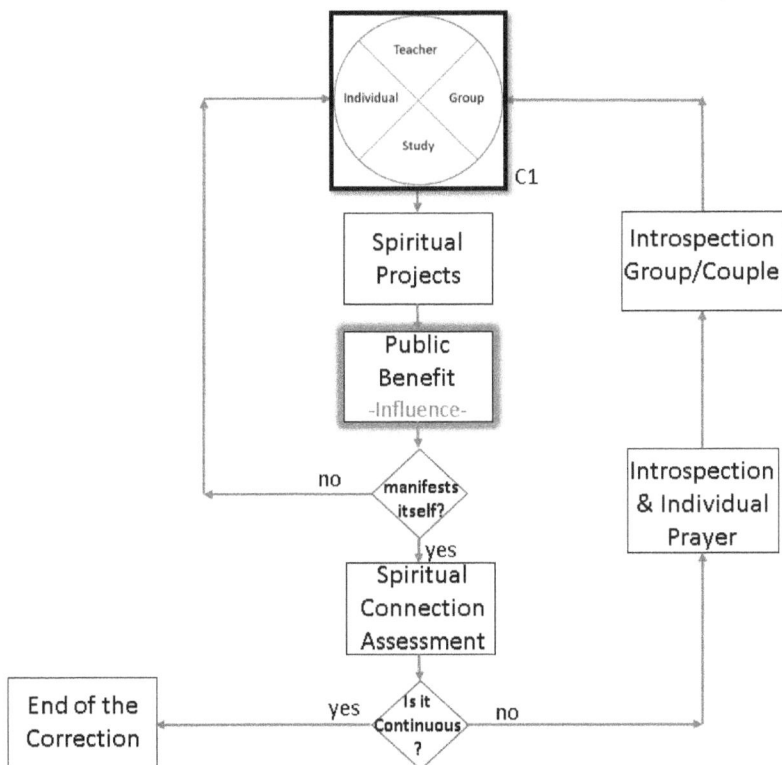

Figure 6

In Figure 7 we show a summary of the entities in Circle II synthesizing Figure 6.

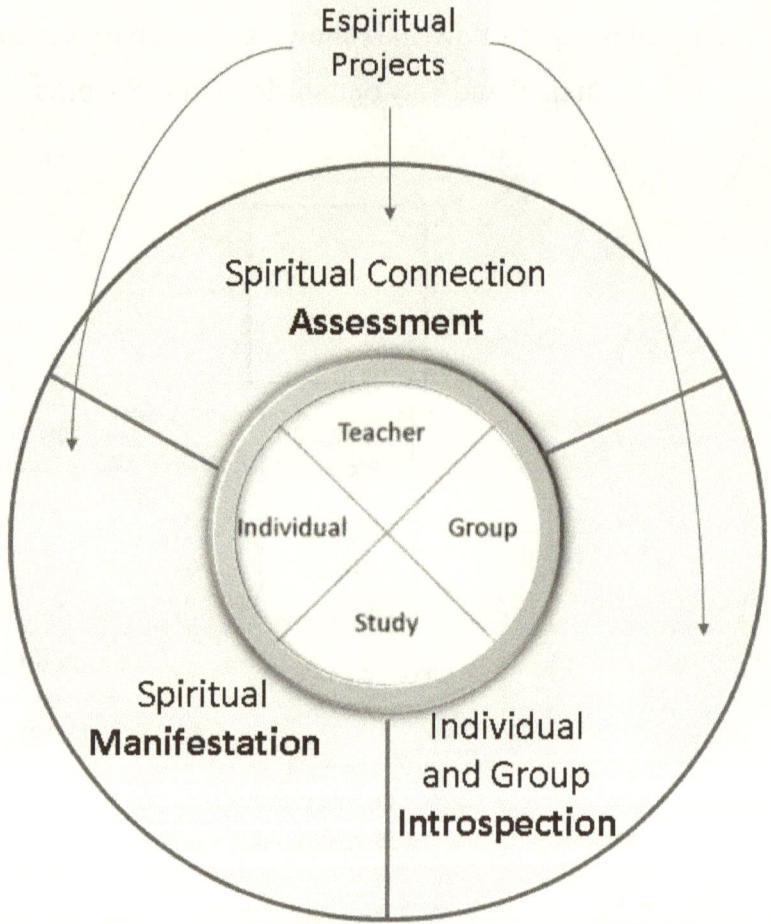

Espiritual
Projects

Spiritual Connection
Assessment

Teacher

Individual   Group

Study

Spiritual
Manifestation

Individual
and Group
Introspection

Entities of Circle II

Figure 7

Manifestation of the Creator's Essence in Us

When our spiritual reality is manifested in the form of influence, dedication, and help, whether it be individually, with a partner, or as a team, we experience a feeling of satisfaction (*sipúk*, in Hebrew). We can see and understand that we are influencing and doing things with a clear dedication to our surroundings, that is, a dedication to others and to the social environment. It may be that we have a motive related to personal convenience or that we will gain something by influencing and giving of ourselves, but it doesn't matter. The important thing is that we are able to help and to contribute to the spiritual cause.

There are two levels of influence or dedication:

a) Being motivated to or having an interest in influencing, and

b) Influencing, giving, committing, and helping purely to do the right thing, what is asked for, what is required, at a higher, altruistic level.

The path needed to ascend sometimes includes returning to start a level again that we have already reached. The rung on which we find ourselves now is called "the current world," and the next rung is called "the next or higher world," in short: the place we are today + one step= the next world or higher world.

One of the key points for someone who is manifesting their spiritual aspect is to maintain the rhythm of spiritual advance so that the Light is shining continuously. Sometimes we feel that we are connected to a higher energy or Light that makes us feel calm and happy, but it quickly fades away and we are again "disconnected." In these cases we will have to continue to be active in Circle I, in addition to reflecting on and evaluating our spirituality.

Individual Introspection and Adjustment to the Creator Within

Once a person has achieved an advance in their spiritual level, the next step is introspection about their advance (or regression) via study, thought, and, sometimes, prayer as well.

We say that nature is all knowledge, and that it is "dressed" or represented in the materials, that is, the Light itself, "translated" into something physical and tangible, which is measurable.

Nature is the internal part of the individual, expressed and copied outside of them. The spiritual partner or team is also turned into part of nature through their spiritual works and projects.

Spiritual introspection at the level of partners or teams is expressed by adjusting desires that still have not become clearly defined. Desires with a better and higher resolution than those with which, for the moment, we are still working. Spiritual introspection is achieved by being honest with ourselves and our partners or teams. With extreme social and emotional care, we have to clarify and air important details without offending or hurting anyone involved in the spiritual project. There's no need to be subordinate to anyone, nor hypocritical, two-faced, or false. With bravery and tact, we should be real and authentic.

In the same way, and as part of the necessary adjustments, we should consider the logistical and organizational coordination of events and situations related to the team or partnership's spiritual work.

It goes without saying that introspection is also related to the social, intellectual, political, and economic interactions of the partnership or team.

Finally, but of fundamental importance: prayer. Whether individual or with a group, all prayer is part of the spiritual system in the process of individual and group introspection.

Evaluating the Spiritual Connection

We should examine our influence on people and on the environment. In this evaluation we quantify the quality and number of "sparks" of the Creator's essence that shine within us.

It's important to evaluate a person's spiritual level or influence. Carrying out spiritual work makes us feel satisfied; it makes us feel fulfilled. This sensation is reflected in a person's Kli, because it has augmented their capacity of spiritual reception. Having a larger Kli also extends the desires, in short, we are growing spiritually.

The individual should continue on until their soul is completely corrected.

We go up a spiritual level according to internal changes that occur within us. External changes don't work, because, as we've seen, everything external is lies and deception; only internal changes exist.

Sometimes an individual can also go backwards in spiritual development, and if this happens to us we should quickly find the lost way again through soliciting, appealing, and praying for our own spiritual well-being and all that is "Israel."

The study of the spiritual system exercises a power over a person. The power is the Light, which acts on the person's spiritual matter. This power is "outside" of us, so we call it a "hidden force." As we have mentioned before, when the Spiritual Light comes over what is hidden, it "illuminates" it and the hidden becomes reveled. When something is clear, something that wasn't manifest before, it's because we have gone up a level. Now we can measure and quantify it.

Every time we are conscious and present, and understand and internalize a spiritual form (a desire), we discover that we have activated the Creator within us expressed in that desire. We say that the desire was latent, because it always existed in us, but it hadn't yet come the Spiritual Light that illuminates it.

Sadly, we let many opportunities for spiritual growth pass by, whether it is because we aren't aware in those moments, or because we don't understand this new spiritual form, a latent desire now implemented, in which our souls acquires new "clothing." When we miss opportunities, we begin to accumulate delays or a reduction in the amount of required Spiritual Light in us. In other words, our desires stay far from being resolved without the Spiritual Light being able to illuminate them. It's a shame to let them pass by, one after another, without understanding them, and therefore far from shining like the Creator.

These delays, accumulated over time (hundreds or thousands of years), translate into prohibitions, violations, opposition, obstacles, restrictions, censorship, and "blows." The blows may be psychological (confusion, dissociation, schizophrenia, etc.), social and physical (all types of sickness, wars, social instability, and also death).

Results and Practice of the Spiritual Model

There are three basic factors to keep in mind to evaluate the results and manifestation of spiritual growth, specifically:

1) The person, group, or couple's spiritual level;
2) The direct recipients or beneficiaries of the project; and
3) The needs and desires satisfied by the spiritual project.

Here is a formula that measures our influence, comprised by with three factors; each factor multiplies the next and gives a result.

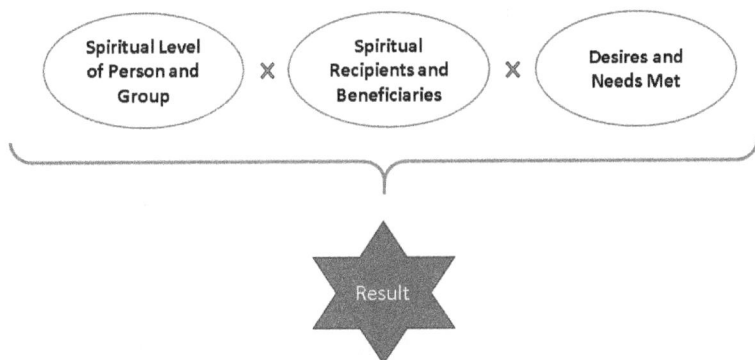

Influence Formula

Figure 8

The Creator, who is "one, unique, and immutable," has the maximum influence. In Him, and I say so in a figurative sense, is the maximum result.

Spiritual Level

When I say spiritual level, I'm referring to that of a person, partnership, or group. All entities have a spiritual Kli. The size of the Kli is the spiritual level.

Achieving a spiritual advance isn't sufficient to maintain it. It is achieved as a result of the spiritual relationship between our self and another person or people, and this should be continuous and constant. Although we experience small ups and downs, we will continue to be aware that we have reached a "new world" with a luxury of details and intensity in every moment which before we did not pause to experience.

It can also be the case that, despite being fully involved in the practice and development of the spiritual system, we do something that makes us lose a level we had achieved. We will notice the difference clearly. From personal experience, I can say that returning to a higher level where we've been goes much faster than reaching that level for the first time. This correction requires introspection of us. It's vital to identify the action or deed that, according to us, diminished our resolution and influence. Once the "drop" is internalized, we can quickly recover our earlier level. We will continue our spiritual work, which will return us to our former level or perhaps even help us reach a higher, more refined level. Continuity is measured in terms of days, weeks, months, etc. With a modest spiritual advance, which we feel constantly and continually, we can do an evaluation of our spiritual state and connection.

Beneficiaries and Recipients of Spiritual Work

The beneficiaries and recipients of the spiritual project are a fundamental factor in the result. "Beneficiaries", and we put in quotation marks because those who do the spiritual work obviously benefit greatly simply from the act of helping or influencing others.

There are direct and indirect beneficiaries or recipients. We won't go into the definition of the types of recipients, but the idea is that they exist and they express some type of "gain" from the spiritual work.

In absolute terms, this being one of the multiplicative factors in our formula, the more direct beneficiaries there are, the better the result.

But it is important to clarify that the number of people who benefit is directly linked to quality and content of the spiritual project. Sometimes, helping a single person in need is equal to or greater than a project that benefits ten people with other necessities or desires.

Satisfying Needs or Desires

The desires or needs satisfied by the spiritual work comprise another fundamental factor in the formula for calculating the spiritual result. The more desires satisfied for a person or group, the better the result.

For this factor we should also make clear that, depending on the type of desire or need, as well as its reach or magnitude, as mentioned before under certain circumstances satisfying one need or desire can generate a result as large as or larger than satisfying many needs or desires together.

This factor can be different for each individual, and their needs or desires can have different weight or importance.

Chapter 9. Perspectives on the Spiritual Model

To explain and develop some points in the proposed spiritual model, we'll present three different perspectives:

1. The tactical perspective
2. The road to transformation
3. The transcendental meaning

To facilitate understanding, we'll use simple spiritual terms and we'll discuss these points of view through questions and answers.

1. The Tactical Perspective

A) *How can the spiritual model be discovered and understood by doing the activities in the Circles described in the last chapter?*

The steps in the spiritual model are relatively simple, but each requires various activities that must be done alone, in a binary relationship with a partner or with the individual in association for society itself.

There's a saying that says that when the student is ready, the teacher will come. The process can be started simply by reading a book about spirituality (it could be this book you're reading now) which awakens a person's curiosity that activates their "point in the heart." From there the reader, with help from the leader and/or their teammates, will be able to begin searching for more texts on the topic in order to gradually find answers for their spiritual needs and desires. Just like the physical and physiological systems in the human body, a person's spiritual system must be fed and kept in good shape.

When a person is consciously imbued with spirituality and learning to manage their spiritual system, the energy they emit attracts more people who are going through similar or complementary states, which will help with their understanding and spiritual practice, until they come to have influence over others.

B) Who should my leader or teacher be?

The spiritual environment for an individual's development should be formed of a teacher or leader, a circle of spiritual companions, books, and study. We must emphasize that choosing our environment is of the highest importance to spiritual growth. An individual's daily life should be framed by a positive spiritual environment, complemented by acts of kindness toward others.

The teacher and leader is someone who, by using the raw materials within each person, teaches them to control the capacity for love and devotion. The teacher is the person who helps us to introduce understanding of spirituality. When the time comes to choose our leader we must pay attention and learn to listen to the desires of our hearts. When we are aware of our reality and present in it, the heart expresses itself clearly. No one should interfere or influence our decisions.

The student must be able to connect to the teacher, just as an embryo is attached to the mother; if this attachment doesn't occur, there will be no possibility of advancing and it would be better for the student to find another teacher.

Students should be responsible and devote themselves to study. Although a student might be very intelligent and have great capacity, if they don't work hard on their studies, if they are negligent or don't follow the teacher's spirit in detail, it will be too difficult to come to any spiritual fulfillment.

And if we truly want to advance spiritually, the best way is to trust in ourselves; we should choose the source of knowledge for ourselves. We should each choose, independently and without pressure, the teacher or leader who answers our questions, satisfies our expectations, and obviously, who is capable of guiding us on the path of spiritual growth.

Once the leader or teacher has been chosen, we are obligated to receive only their spiritual instruction, and not pay attention to anyone else. After all, we are going to develop spiritually, and it is counterproductive for a person to hear contradictory doctrines during their spiritual growth.

C) *Is there a particular way to complete the spiritual model's interpersonal activities that is best?*

The majority of interpersonal relationships consist, basically, of a relationship at the intellection, social, economic, and, sometimes, emotional level.

Usually, there is an interaction between two minds, without there being communion or communication between them at the spiritual level. This type of interaction creates conflict in relationships. When the mind and intellect controls us, problems aren't far behind.

When we're conscious of our body and mind, without influence from past feelings nor expectations of the future, with a "clean" mind present in the moment we're living,that is when our interpersonal relationships and spiritual projects can be fruitful.

D) *How should one choose a spiritual team, partner, or soul-friend?*

There aren't predetermined rules for choosing a team of
spiritual companions or a spiritual friend. This varies from
culture to culture and country to country, according to the
mentality and customs of the area. It also varies according to
social and economic status, gender, education, and level of
equality in the society in which they live. Choosing just men,
just women, or a mixture, as well as other factors, can
influence the choice.

Sometimes it's a good idea to do psychological activities with
experts which will quickly identify the different types of
person so they can be classified and divided into compatible
groups.

The main thing, when choosing a spiritual friend or partner is
that they be already aware of their "point in the heart" or are
close to manifesting and recognizing it. By being conscious of
our present we can clearly visualize the union with our
partner, so that every activity we undertake maintains and
constantly elevates our spiritual level. In this way, with each
step and shared event the spiritual relationship gets more
and more refined, like someone adjusting the focus on
binoculars, until they are on the way to a single spiritual
reality, sharing experiences together. It's important to clarify
that if a partnership is already established, it's not necessary

for them to be physically together all the time. The mutual spiritual project exists and continues to develop as it is being worked on, although the people may not be together physically. The same is true when people are communicating by phone, internet, social media, or using smartphone apps in real time.

When people find themselves in a spiritual collective, it's important to emphasize that joint study—students and teachers—should take place in a specific location. Just as a fetus is isolated inside the mother's womb, the soul of a person in the process of spiritual growth and development needs to be protected and sheltered. We should be surrounded by love, attention, and care like a baby. A healthy atmosphere should be created to surround us.

While students haven't yet reached any revelations about the spiritual system, they won't have a very clear understanding of what is happening. They feel thrown back and forth from one state to another, fragile with knowledge, with new theories and concepts about the spiritual system inside them. During the "construction" process we are exposed to unstable, occasionally ethereal states. We can compare these feelings to Noah's ark, in which Noah, his family, and all the animals lived isolated for an entire year, until the water went

down, the ark ran aground on Mount Ararat and they came
out onto to dry land.

As a result, we shouldn't expose ourselves to external factors
except for the leader of our spiritual community.

> E) *Are there methods or strategies based on the spiritual*
> *model that we could use to manage the present*
> *correctly, conscious and with presence, living in the now*
> *in the optimal way?*

Coming to a state of consciousness and being focused on the
now is to be conscious of oneself, of our existence, and the
needs of others.

There are various methods to manage our egos so that they
do not take control of our minds. At the minimal possibility of
this occurring, the danger must be immediately overcome,
because we run the risk of falling into depression and that,
which is caused by our mind and our own ego, would drown
us and lead to our destruction.

The methods used to reach and maintain a state of presence
vary and depend on what works or is most comfortable for
each individual.

2. The Road to Transformation

A) If we follow the activities of the spiritual model, is there some type of transformation of the individual or group as a result of subscribing to the spiritual system?

The steps and activities do influence how the individual behaves alone, in partnership, or in a team. Each one of us has our own vision of the world we live in. We perceive it differently every time, and as we change our attributes and characteristics of spiritual perception, we recognize that personal transformation is necessary and it's not the world that needs to change.

The spiritual force that is received when we join a team of people in a spiritual project gives us the resources and the reach to bring correction to the world. There isn't a stronger or greater force than spiritual unity.

B) How can we motivate and inspire others?

Basically, we must accept ourselves as we are. Any of our qualities (ambition, laziness, kindness, sympathy, etc.) will be exercised for good once our connection with others, mutual understanding and guarantee and interdependence are received and internalized.

All of our desires or characteristics—for example, achieving something, envying someone, being energetic or lazy, playing clean or cheating—are internal impulses that are latent within us and are an integral part of our personal texture. Correcting or criticizing them doesn't help at all because, though they might be dealt with and put aside temporarily, in the end they will come to the surface again.

But simply by having the intention and enthusiasm to complete a spiritual project and get closer to others, to join and be in internal coordinated harmony in the team, the characteristics or qualities of each are connected, through which the group grows spiritually. Many of our desires, once they join the desires of the group, fit in such a way that the most important qualities for the spiritual project and the ones that benefit the whole group come to the fore.

The fact that the Kli of a collective can now take care of needs that before each person couldn't even consider as an individual is a source of motivation and inspiration for all.

C) *How can we know that our spirituality is active, progressing, and reaching more and more intense levels of influence?*

Spiritual growth means increasing our sensitivity and the internal identification of our desires. The spiritual system is measured by its quality and intensity, not its quantity. In other words, as we progress to a more intense spiritual level, all experiences become sharper and more refined.

We don't become stronger or more insensitive, but rather enjoy an observational ability that penetrates deeper, scrutinizes in more detail, and is more sensitive to things. Likewise, when before we felt nothing, now we begin to perceive new qualities and events that we didn't expect and that we used to pass by without focusing on, without detailing them, or understanding them, or gaining any advantage from them. We start to have a feeling of oh! and aha! at the sensation of being amazed by something that happens.

The idea is that through the advance in our understanding of the spiritual system we become capable of continually becoming more profound, to recognize and simplify our internal qualities more and more, and analyze the world around us in more detail.

The Kli of each person who is progressing in spirituality expands and begins to reveal new things and awareness about the world around us. Part of the person's Kli gets woven in with the Kelim of the members of the spiritual team, to include more and more people—although they don't yet belong to the group—until they cover our entire reality. In this way we come to mutually influence each person and each of their worlds, until we create a system of interconnected external worlds inside an internal web of souls which can act like one larger, and more powerful soul.

> D) *Does love in a spiritual relationship help us to change the type and meaning of our intimate relationships as a couple?*

In a spiritual connection, an intimate sexual relationship between two people becomes a physiological expression of that harmony. If there is no spiritual connection, there's no incentive or motive for a physical connection; it would only be a hormonal or merely carnal attraction.

So why do we feel happy when there is love between a couple? What do we get that makes us smile? The reality is that we don't get anything, but what makes us happy is rather being able to love and give to another.

The spiritual root of sex is the soul's identification with the essence of the Creator. That is the final goal of nature. Sex, the maximum physical pleasure in this world, is the root of all our desires. We all want to reach this physical union because, in turn, we were created by the union of our parents. In the spiritual world, sex represents a union of opposite desires, with the shared desire to physically please the other.

The sensation and pleasure generated by our sexual-spiritual connection together is the only one in which we find true, lasting pleasure, which transforms the couple.

A single sexual relation has no memory. Once the sexual act is over we cannot describe or remember what the sensation was like, until the next time we have it. The only thing that remains is the couple's spiritual connection.

E) *Does contact with sacred texts help to transform us into people with a higher spiritual sensibility?*

Reading sacred text sharpens an individual's perception of the world. These texts, in general, are impossible to internalize using the mind. They can only be understood and put into practice by correcting the soul. The commentaries written by Kabbalistic sages help students to discover what is written in the texts and to attract the Spiritual Light. Paradoxically, it's impossible to know the spiritual world until we are capable of perceiving and understanding it within our souls. At root, study is a way to understand how the spiritual world is constructed within us, how our Kli and the Light within it works, or how the Light "dresses" the Kli.

By studying sacred texts we receive the Spiritual Light that helps us to reform and correct our souls. Once the Light is received and the discovery of the events discussed in the book of Zohar begins, the soul itself begins to teach and guide us.

> F) *Are the study of the spiritual system and practice of mutual guarantee what will help us survive and transform the current world?*

Globalization, the internet, smart phones, and other technological advances, framed within a capitalist system, are leading the world to be controlled by supranational companies or entities grouped together in cartels or corporations with economic power according to the area or industry they specialize in (for example, the finance companies, those that control food, fuel, medicines, etc.). States and nations are showing themselves to be incapable of offering complete solutions and basic services to their people in the 21st century. The people show their discontent with this immense incompetence. There are clear symptoms of the State, in its current conception, disappearing, and we begin to see the composition of a new supranational State with borders that are non-existent or variable.

The constant growth of humanity's ego will continue separating us, fragmenting us, disintegrating societies and turning each of us into independent entities capable of living anywhere in the world, without a need to belong to any society, community, or country, or in the chaos, belonging to all at the same time.

People's survival in the face of this cultural, social, and virtual invasion that threatens the identity of the State, can only be achieved through the practice of mutual guarantee among people who, in turn, will bring us to knowledge and progress in the spiritual system. When we belong to a unified global community whose lowest common denominator is the "point in the heart" of each of its members, we will be able to transform global society.

G) *Do prayer and meditation help us to advance spiritually?*

When we pray we reveal the Creator within ourselves, the dedication and infinite attribute of influence that we carry inside. The Kabbalah explains that prayer is a request to be corrected, because we cannot do it alone.

During prayer we are demanding that the Light correct everything necessary so that we can receive what we desire.

A person's level of spiritual advance affects how effective the prayers are.

Rabbi Yehuda Ashlag says that praying constantly and despairing that we see no answer to our prayers actually brings us nearer to state of happiness, because as a result of so much prayer and supplication we will have finally become worthy of beginning to sincerely ask for the Creator's help. We should note that egotistical prayers don't attract Spiritual Light; they only have a certain psychological effect on the person praying.

The texts of the prayers come from sacred books. These prayers have been written in books of prayers established by sages. The act of prayer brings us closer to the essence of the Creator, although we may not understand what is written. The result of the prayer or reading depends entirely on the reader, not on the text, nor its author.

As for meditation, it is a method of internal analysis based on observations of our characteristics and intentions. There are many approaches, styles, schools, and trainings about how to meditate. In many religions mediation uses letters, phrases, or images, and is related to relaxation and maintaining emotional equilibrium or other psychological goals.

The need to feel the universe within us has led to meditation methods that allow one to "leave" physical matter behind and rise above it, or in other words, one has an out-of-body experience.

The topic of meditation and prayer will be covered in more depth in a separate work.

> H) *How does having a spiritual team benefit our*
> *transformation?*

First, joining a spiritual collective offers the opportunity to gain new friendships in the world of spirituality.

The Light is able to influence each person in the group and counteract the egotistical nature of each through study and debate. During a connection among people whose "points in the heart" are already awake, the Light of correction begins to appear in each heart. Then, as they are present and conscious during the various team activities, they will begin to see their own progress and the Spiritual Light flowing within them.

It's important to clarify that the Light is everywhere, all the time. A spiritual collective—which is now a receptive Kli— begins to distinguish, to be conscious of, to be aware of the Spiritual Light, whereas before this spiritual union they did not feel, nor were they conscious of it. The Spiritual light is constant. We only need to want to receive it.

By becoming an integral part of a spiritually-inclined society, each of its members receives the unified force of the entire collective, which represents the power of the common soul of all of them. This means that each person's aspiration turns into a larger desire for the Light than the individual would have alone. Being part of a team also creates a defense against influences from the outside world, which can be resisted more easily.

3. Transcendental Meaning

A) *How can we improve our world based on our spiritual conscience and that of the group?*

Studying the book of the Zohar and other sacred texts of Kabbalah gives us the formulas and techniques for living in abundance, peace, health, and happiness. Cooperation among people who act out of common spiritual desire can achieve this purpose.

This cooperation is not to connect bodies, thoughts, and words, but rather for people's understanding of the spiritual system, which, in turn, puts us on the path to a true human society, constructed for the common good, the spiritual project which is bigger than all its members and is above us. We can clearly see that nature is integrated into a perfect, balanced system, at the mineral, vegetable, and animal levels. The only missing component needed to maintain this equilibrium is human beings, who, for the moment, are absent, and on the contrary, threaten nature and the environment more and more.

When our spiritual unity is articulated, we will encounter perfect, beautiful harmony at all levels of nature. That is the final stage of our evolution in the current world conditions. Humanity's spiritual path today is, for now: to be born, grow up, reproduce, and die, generation after generation, until we can solidly build a common spiritual desire which will one day be a single one which accepts all our desires.

B) *How can society be better served at both the individual and collective levels?*

Everything starts with children. How they are raised is fundamental to their development and contribution to society. Children, from the moment they go to Kindergarten and later on to high school, should begin to be part of a

society based on appropriate teaching about the spiritual
system for each child and their spiritual community.

Starting in childhood, we should teach children to appreciate
life at a more abstract level. We should make them aware that
there is much more in the world than what we can see, touch,
smell, taste, and hear. Through games and examples, we can
easily help them to identify the hidden forces that control
reality and make up part of the spiritual system. When the
child understands the basic fundamentals of giving,
supporting, collaborating, and love, they will likewise enjoy
and appreciate knowing how to live in peace and harmony
with the environment, adapting themselves to universal
balance in spite of their egotistical natures.

As we've seen, to live in a society of mutual guarantee is to
serve it based on the solid foundation of a collective spiritual
model connected to its basic values.

C) *How can we shape our children so they act morally and
   ethically, so they will gain more satisfaction and better
   results from any activity?*

As the Kabbalah says, education has nothing to do with age, it
has no start or finish. Education is the same for us, the adults,
as it is for our children. The difference is that for children we
use tools appropriate for their level of mental and emotional

understanding. We, the adults, can also learn alongside them and from them.

Education is the path everyone follows from infancy to old age. As parents, we hope to inculcate values in our children that will guide them towards the right path, we hope they will be successful in everything and serve the community and country well. Education should help young people to discover the causes that govern the world and life.

Ensuring a better future for our children means raising them in a healthy environment, sharing a spiritual team and with the goal of living in harmony with the environment, love for creation and all its expressions, and disinterested dedication to others. We never forget that both adults and children are products of their socio-economic, cultural, and physical environment.

Children must be treated with respect for their own lives, with importance, always telling them the truth, answering all their questions and listening to their suggestions, being cautious and considerate, advising them honestly, and approaching them as friends.

> D) *Given the precarious current position of the global economy, an irreparable climate, and a fragile ecosystem deteriorating constantly, how can*

improvement for our planet come out of studying and
understanding the spiritual system?

Western capitalism is based on a perpetually growing economy. Without growth, there is no stability in the capitalist system. With this economic model of growth and development, we are very far from supplying the basic needs of the world population. The system has produced our current problems. Both in Western countries and in the majority of those in Latin America, Africa, and Asia, there are millions or unemployed or under-employed people, people who are homeless or displaced, on top of hundreds of daily bankruptcies, businesses which did not achieve "growth" and are absorbed by private conglomerates which, grouped into cartels, are defended by politicians, panicked by their impotence, ineptitude, and the impossibility of managing the global crisis.

We don't intend to start a debate about capitalism, nor how we can improve it. This isn't about replacing it either, as free enterprise, its base, is in many ways positive and necessary for modern society's development. Free enterprise and creativity are natural to humans. Free enterprise, based on a positive spiritual project, will benefit humanity. What we can help with is correcting the ravages and aberrations of the capitalist system through large-scale spiritual projects, in order to gradually reach the minimum required to live with honor, health, and decency, satisfied with the present.

The positive side of the unstable global condition—because there is no bad that does not result in good, and as we've noted several times, there's something good in everything—is that people's desperation and dissatisfaction will lead us, sooner or later, to create a new type of socio-economic organization for the whole planet.

The ecosystem doesn't depend directly on us, but the economic system does, and this, in turn, directly affects the ecosystem. A socio-economic change is vital, both at the local and global level, as is a change in our intentions from "receive for ourselves" to "give of myself to others."

The only possible way is to separate, understand, and manage our egotistical nature and make room for an opposite quality: the Spiritual Light, which will change us into maximal benefactors, givers, contributors, helpers, counselors, and influencers.

Participating in spiritual projects helps us to fulfill our desire to have influence, but each project needs to follow norms and limits which contribute to improving the ecosystem, without impoverishing the present.

The greatest social, community, and global challenge is raising the awareness of authorities who, in turn, defend to the death the status quo and are not interested in changing their mentalities. There are many ways to explain this behavior, because it's contrary to their capitalist definition. The current system, including banking, industry, securities, business conglomerates, politicians and governments, will continue to inject trillions of dollars and putting the people in debt up to their eyebrows to maintain government inertia and, obviously, to avoid anyone talking about a crisis.

People's situation is comparable to sophisticated slavery and powerlessness, maintained by propaganda through the consumption of unnecessary articles, whose pressure to buy the latest-model cars or to be fashionable is permanent and exhausting. If we believe we are working to support our families, we are fundamentally mistaken: we work to support the ever-voracious consumer system.

The solution is an economy in which consumption is reasonable and provides the basic necessities for life, such as food, housing, social security, health care, work, recreation, and formal and spiritual education, in a way that is sensible and appropriate for everyone.

A new cultural and socio-economic agreement would bring with it an age of transition in which everyone would emphasize a new vision of spiritual characteristics. Those in power should show their clear will to change and begin to actively implement it at all levels. Until this happens, we should tolerate the current system, and work with the authorities to prevent a complete collapse of the current system and avoid chaos, until the new society and socio-spiritual system begins to work. This is a broad theme and merits further discussion on another forum.

> E) *Does understanding the spiritual system influence our ability to move from level to level until we obtain the influence of the Creator's essence?*

Knowledge of the spiritual system does influence everyone positively and progressively more and more in each of the spiritual fields and elements: ourselves as individuals and as a group.

As we advance from level to level, our influence on the team and the team's influence on us grows exponentially and proportionally to our Kli's reception of the Spiritual Light. The Creator, source of our souls and whose essence is an intrinsic part of our spiritual DNA, becomes more clearly and intensely evident in all our relationships and connections with our partners, family, and society.

F) What is our obligation to the world we live in?

All souls are united in a single spiritual system, in a universal soul. By studying spirituality, we create positive energy in the cosmos, affecting the entire universe. This way, with just the union into groups and among groups, it's possible to push the world toward change. When we establish the correct system of spiritual relationships among each of us, this will impact the world we live in. This work is our priority and responsibility which, with the help of the Creator, we come to be very soon. Amen.

Once we live in a state of mutual guarantee, we will feel a degree of complete harmony that becomes more and more perfect. Each of us will acquire the right to connect ourselves to a higher level, one of a higher quality, more intense existence. Then we will reach a state in which we don't simply inhabit a biological body, but rather, in addition, we live and feel emotions and the mind to a human degree and level.

In this way, we will achieve the reality of superior perception that is eternal and perfect, ascending to a level at which everything is more elevated than at the level of animation we experience.

Sometimes the world flows gradually and changes spiritually to be conscious of this change of perception of the world. In the study and practice of the proposed spiritual model, we suddenly become conscious and become more perceptive and alert. We understand more intensely some things that we couldn't before, and each of us experiences a rise in consciousness. This state is stimulated by the idea of unity and being conscious of the need to change. The Spiritual Light of reform and correction becomes active in every person. It is not mundane knowledge that is developed, but the presence of the Spiritual Light and its harmonious union with the universal Kli. This is the path that we must open to humanity with our union.

Examples of Spiritual Projects

Below we list some examples of spiritual projects.

At the individual level, consider these options:

- Help elderly people and people with social, intellectual, or emotional disabilities.
- Support students with limited resources financially.
- Offer business consulting to benefit minority groups.

- Offer financial help to people with limited resources or people whose low incomes do not cover their basic necessities.

- Loan money without intent to profit to help start a business to pull someone out of the cycle of poverty.

- Organize youth clubs for extracurricular education and offer logistical and financial support.

- Create jobs for people who, for any reason, have difficulty finding well paid jobs to cover their basic living expenses.

- Volunteer for or create organizations that help to solve car trouble, for free, available through a simple phone call or click on an app. This type of organization already exists in Israel.

At the Community level, these are some examples:

- Construct buildings for public benefit with free service, to be used by libraries, hospitals, sports complexes, meeting rooms, parks, and public spaces.

- Help immigrant, refugee, or displaced families with their social adaptation.

At the social level:

- Therapy offered by psychologists or social workers to communities and individuals experiencing crisis.

- Nonprofit groups to offer social and financial support to people with identified needs or physical limitations.
- Free post-secondary education for adults about spiritual projects of public benefit.
- Low-cost recreation and social options for local people.
- Economic stimulus and encouragement for research and development in areas that benefit the community.
- Training on how run an ethical, socially responsible, and environmentally-friendly business.

At the national and governmental level:

- Socially-beneficial laws: high-quality education and health care for low-income people.
- Promoting programs that raise well-being.
- Eliminate bureaucracy as much as possible, both in the State and the independent corporations that impact our daily lives.
- Humanize how people are treated by bureaucracies. Serve the public with love and for the good of the customer or user of any service.
- Laws to conserve the ecosystem and for local and global ecological balance of environmental resources

(clean air, unpolluted rivers, potable water, unpolluted soil, sound at a level that is not harmful to hearing, etcetera.)

- Education and publicity on health, nutrition, and spiritual topics.
- Real, full financing for families without homes, without interest or commission which multiply the original value of the building at ridiculous costs for people with limited or no income.
- Real price control in the areas of housing, food, services and primary, secondary, and university education.
- Fair treatment of animals and appropriate management of natural resources.

At the global level:

- Eradication of sicknesses like malaria, Ebola, HIV, and other plagues or viruses with global impact.
- Welcoming refugees, social and financial support for those displaced for political or economic reasons, by wars, persecution and natural disasters.
- Universal anticontamination laws and harsh global sanctions for those who pollute the environment. Imposing fines directly proportional to the health and

insurance costs of those directly affected by the
poisoned air, water, and other natural resources.

Acknowledgements

I confess I feel lucky to have met hundreds of people—friends, and acquaintances—on my path, from whom I've learned many life lessons, including their spiritual points of view. It's almost impossible to name so many people, but I want to mention my parents, teachers, classmates, family, friends, colleagues, bosses, rabbis, experts, and many others who offered me their generous attention. I thank all of them from the bottom of my heart.

I owe gratitude to many people. Here I'll only name a few of my most recent teachers who stand out for their dedication, patience, and devotion to the study of the Zohar and the secrets of the Kabbalah: Rabbi Rafael Granot and Hyam Beker.

I'm also thankful for the valuable comments from my brother, Dr. Isaac Aizenman, and for my wife, Avital (Tali), my daughter, Rivka, and my friend Ralph Resnik.

Bibliography

I read and studied a great deal, and there were uncountable classes, conferences, and seminars which I attended over the years. I will only list the main sources for the creation of this book.

- *Introduction to the book of Zohar*, by Rabbi Yehuda Halevy Ashlag, the Baal Hasulam
- *Preface to the book of Zohar*, by the Baal Hasulam
- *The Zohar*, by Rabbi Shimon Bar Yohai (with explication by Baal Hasulam)
- Kabbalah *for the Student*, by Dr. Michael Laitman
- *Anatomy of the Soul from Rebbe Najman of Breslov*, by Haim Kramer
- *The Power of Now*, by Eckhart Tolle
- *Introduction to the study of the Ten Sefirot,* by the Baal Hasulam
- *Primary to the knowledge of Kabbalah* , by the Baal Hasulam
- *Talmud of the Ten Sefirot*, by the Baal Hasulam
- *Meditation and Kabbalah,* by Aryeh Kaplan

Glossary of Terms

Aliá – rise, spiritual ascent

Altruism – the act of doing something so another person gets direct satisfaction

Arvút – mutual guarantee

Beshert – twin souls

Biná - understanding

Bushá – shame, embarrassment

Creation – process the Creator used to create the spiritual and material world.

Creator – universal source of Spiritual Light, unitary, unique, and immutable, there is no other outside Him; in Hebrew, *Boreh*

Daat - knowledge

Dinim – plural of din, impediments, judgements, laws, edicts

Double Concealment– not being conscious of not having the tools to discover the Creator

Ego – desire to feel pleasure or satisfaction with a sense of personal identity.

Ex nihilo – something created out of nothing

Gevurá - judgement

Guf – body, realm of desire

Heichal – premises, realm of desire

Hod - splendor

Infinite – first step before of Creation

Integrated Ego – humanity's common ego

Chayá – essence, living soul

Chésed - kindness

Chochmá - wisdom

Kelim - plural of Kli

Keter - crown

Kli – recipient, cup, vessel, receptor body and host for the Spiritual Light

Levush – clothing, realm of desire

Malchut – kingdom

Milúi – full, fulfilled

Mitzva – singular of the word mitzvot

Mitzvot – acts of kindness

Nájat rúach – bestowing and spreading pleasure and pride

Néfesh – Resident soul

Neshamá – divine soul, breath, realm of desire

Netzach - victory

Rachamim – mercy, compassion

Reshimó – impression of the Spiritual Light that is recorded in the Kli, spiritual DNA

Root – realm of desire, in Hebrew: shoresh

Rúach - spirit

Sacred Scriptures – Tanach, Mishná, Talmud, Zohar, Ecclesiastes, Book of Lamentations, Psalms

Sefirot – Emanations, shining rays, or attributes of the Spiritual Light

Shabat – Saturday in English, the seventh day of the week in Judaism, day of rest

Shoresh – root, realm of desire

Simple Concealment– being conscious of lacking the tools to discover the creator

Sipuk – pleasure, satisfaction

Soul - spiritual part of a person, energy, force, or desire for spirituality; breath of desire, in Hebrew: *neshamá*

Spiritual DNA – the Carrier of an individual's spiritual genetic information. Spiritual DNA is also responsible for transmission and emergence of the information.

Spiritual Light – intangible force or energy which comes to the world and to humanity

Spirituality – expression of the "divine" aspect within us that acts as an influence on others in reciprocal conditions of mutual responsibility.

The Point in the Heart – desire for spirituality

<u>Tiferet</u> – beauty

<u>Universal Kli</u> – the collective Kli of everyone on planet Earth

<u>Universal Soul</u> – soul of all of humanity, the soul of Adam, the first man.

<u>Yejidá</u> – unique essence, soul

<u>Yesod</u> - foundation

<u>Zeir-anpin</u> – Little face, group of six sefirot

<u>Zohar</u> – Splendor (sacred book)

The Author

Abraham was born and raised in Colombia, and currently lives in Israel. In the exact sciences, Abraham has 40 years of experience in IT and holds a degree in Computer Science from the Technion Institute of Israel and a Masters in Mathematics from Waterloo University, Canada. In the humanities and arts, Abraham studied film at Ryerson University, Toronto, Canada.

Abraham has seemingly opposite but complementary properties: he's spiritual, idealistic, artistic, and sensitive to nature with an excellent power of abstraction, but he is also realistic and has his feet on the ground. He is disciplined, methodical, precise and immune to fantasy. Abraham has things in common with Don Quixote but also with Sancho Panza, as Leonor Uribe Jospeh wrote to Abraham in her youth in a poem, "You are made of a cold heat, a relieving ardor. You are made of contrasts, intense extremism, made of sun and wind. You are a boy and an elder, intense or a pale reflection..."

For more than 25 years, he has explored esoteric themes, specifically in the area of Kabbalah.

Abraham has published articles in different subjects and languages. He is fluent in English, Hebrew and Spanish.

Abraham directed, wrote and produced short films, one of which, *Beshert (The Soul Mate)*, participated in several international film festivals, winning a prize at one. *Beshert* is a love story based on the Kabbalah. Abraham writes and maintains two websites with news of Israel, one in English (www.todaynewsline.com) and one in Spanish (www.infopublico.com).

Abraham began to ask himself if there was something that, without having physical mass or magnetism, communicated between or united people. If there was a system which, though imperceptible to our five senses, exists and unites us all, no matter how far apart people are physically, not limited by time or space, which we could call a "spiritual system."

Abraham is sharing his accumulated knowledge, notes and advice for those on the path to spirituality.

Abraham brings us in this, his first book, a structured method to help us to recognize and to manage the spiritual system of each of us explaining in general terms the spiritual composition of a person, his spiritual DNA.

Email: aaizenm@gmx.com

Web: www.abrahamaizenman.com

www.ingramcontent.com/pod-product-compliance
Lightning Source LLC
Chambersburg PA
CBHW031252090426
42742CB00007B/417